ON CAMERA
How to produce film and video

On Camera

How to produce film and video

Harris Watts

BRITISH BROADCASTING CORPORATION

First published in 1982 as
The Programme-Maker's Handbook,
or *Goodbye Totter TV*
by Starstream Books

This revised and expanded edition
published in 1984 by the
British Broadcasting Corporation,
35 Marylebone High Street
London W1M 4AA

ISBN 0 563 20268 8

Illustrated by Bryan Reading
Printed in Great Britain at
The Pitman Press, Bath

Contents

for Christina, Jonathan, Matthew, Lucy and Amy

My thanks

to Yousuf Aziz, Andrew Quicke, Murray Thomsett and Chris Whiteley who read the parts dealing with their speciality and told me where I was going wrong . . .

to Rob Wright who gave me the benefit of his editing and teaching experience . . .

to Ken Shepheard of BBC Television who read the whole book twice and corrected and encouraged me . . .

to Eddie Iroh, novelist and Controller of Documentary Programmes in Lagos, Nigeria, who gave me the idea in the first place . . .

to Ed Boyce of BBC Television Training for his patient briefings on video technology . . .

to Gordon Croton, Head of BBC Television Training, without whom there would be no *On Camera* book or tapes . . .

and to all those people who answered my questions when I was learning and asked me questions when I was teaching.

**On Camera –
The BBC Video
Production Course**

On Camera – the BBC Video Production Course, written and produced by Harris Watts – is a joint venture between the BBC's Television Training Department and BBC Enterprises Ltd, offering for the first time an integrated course designed to help you use film and video more effectively.

The course is aimed at the wide range of institutional users who may find themselves involved in programme production for the first time, be it the recording of the Chairman's Annual Report, the production of a training programme for new staff, or planning programmes for a community access slot on the local cable channel. This course will provide the basic introduction you need.

The BBC Video Production Course consists of three elements:

– this book, which provides you with an overall introduction to the subject.

– four videocassettes (available on any format) covering the following four topics:

1 The Camera

2 Planning a programme

3 Interviews

4 Editing

– four specially written leaflets accompanying the videocassettes which provide more detailed explanations of each topic and offer suggestions for follow-up exercises.

The videocassettes are designed to complement and illustrate the Basics section of this book. Future tapes will provide illustrative material for the Briefing section, and will look, for example, at lenses, lighting and commentary writing in more detail.

Each videocassette and accompanying leaflet is available as an independent unit. Alternatively, all the material can be supplied as a complete set. For details of price and availability, please contact:

BBC Enterprises Ltd
Education and Training Sales
Woodlands
80 Wood Lane.
London W12 0TT

Telephone: 01-743 5588 and 01-576 0202
Telex: 934678 and 265781

About the author

Harris Watts joined the BBC immediately after graduating from Cambridge in 1963 with a degree in Chinese and Economics. He trained and worked as a radio producer for two years and then transferred to BBC television to train and work as a producer/director specialising in topical and science documentaries for programmes such as *Panorama*, *Tomorrow's World* and *Horizon*. He also produced programmes for several British ITV companies and West Germany's ARD network.

He has had a long connection with broadcasters outside Europe. In the mid-sixties he spent over a year (on attachment from the BBC) with educational radio in East Malaysia. From 1977 to 1979 he was Programme Production Manager for Brunei television.

NOTE:
The San Totta Television Corporation and its staff are pure invention and any resemblance between them and reality should be taken with a large pinch of salt.

Since then he has kept a foot in both camps by combining work as a freelance producer/director in Britain with spells as producer or instructor for the BBC and a growing number of countries such as Nigeria, Libya and Singapore.

This book is based therefore on first-hand experience of both production and teaching.

How to use this book

1   Read through Part One – Basics – quickly, making use of the summaries at the end of each chapter and not paying too much attention to the detail. This will give you a grasp of the principles and procedures you will need to make programmes.

2   Read through the Basics again when you are doing your first few programmes. This time pay more attention to the details and use the summaries to make sure that you haven't forgotten anything important for your programme.

3   Read through the Briefings in Part Two when you are ready for them. They give a detailed explanation of topics – some technical, some not – which will mean more to you when you have had the experience of making one or two programmes.

Foreword by Gordon Croton

Over the last thirty years there have been numerous books written about the techniques of television production – and very few good ones. In many ways this is surprising. After all there has been no shortage of talented and innovative people over the years in British television and some have certainly contrived to leave a definitive mark on the production development of an industry noted for its ephemera. Yet the fact is that many of the books produced by leading practitioners about their approach to the making of television are disappointing. Some are glossily presented and apparently authoritative but in practice contain an uneasy mixture of advice and reminiscence. Others aspire to being technical encyclopedias and emerge from the publisher looking like a cross between a hastily produced telephone directory and Gray's *Anatomy*. There have, of course, been honourable exceptions to this trend, not least the late Desmond Davis's small volume *The Grammar of Television Production* – first published in 1960 and for many years the Bible of the aspiring television producer. Davis wrote his book at the beginning of television's heyday, a time when money for production was freely – perhaps too freely – available and when technical developments in all aspects of studio production were occurring at a great rate. The book is refreshingly straightforward and modest in its aims as it sets out to ensure that 'the beginner who follows the precepts set out in this book will avoid the grosser errors of television production'.

Over twenty years later Desmond Davis's work is out of print and in truth has been overtaken not so much by a reassessment of its principles, as by the technological context in which television is produced. For some years in the BBC's Television Training Department we have been looking for a handbook that would both express the old values – the rules that make for good television – and, at the same time, take account of the constantly changing technological scene. For there is no doubt that a process of demystification has been happening in training for broadcast television production. In earlier days – as I remember well – the television producer too often allowed complex technological processes to elude him and accepted gratefully that they were understood only by technicians who – as often as not – both practised and perpetuated a particular mystique. But the onset of lightweight portable equipment, allied to considerable changes in post-production methods and the sophisticated attitude taken towards technology by new recruits to television, have meant that the training process has changed considerably in the last few years. And with that change has come a need for new support materials. Today, film and video are no longer just the province of the public broadcaster. The range of people and organisations who are in one way or another producing visual materials is constantly growing.

Thus it was that the initial publication of Harris Watts's *The Programme-Maker's Handbook* was particularly welcomed in Television Training Department. To find a book that embodied most of the 'do's and don'ts' of television and at the same time encompassed positive briefings, useful hints and hard-nosed revision was a happy chance. We tried it on our own students – aspiring directors in film and studio – and were not really surprised to find that it soon became an indispensable *vade mecum*. A year later, with new material added and a certain amount of rewriting suggested by staff and students, I am particularly pleased to introduce the book as a BBC publication under its new title *On Camera – How to produce film and video*.

Gordon Croton
Head of Television Training
BBC-TV

Introduction to the Second Edition

This book was first published in 1982 with the title *The Programme-Maker's Handbook or Goodbye Totter TV*. Its reception was heartwarming: reviewers praised it, TV companies and the public bought it, training schools – notably the BBC's – adopted it as a standard textbook. This reissue marks a second phase in its life – as the core of BBC Television Training's integrated course of videocassettes and print entitled *On Camera – the BBC Video Production Course*.

The setting for the book may have changed, but within the covers the arrangement is the same. The first part of the book, *Basics*, has been written with a location shoot in mind, but most of the points apply to studio programmes as well. In fact, ideas, research, imagination and preparation are even more important in the studio, where the producer has total control over variables such as light, weather, sound and scenery, than on location, where he does not. Chapter Eleven explains production procedures which are special to studio programmes. Chapter Twelve discusses techniques for outside broadcasts.

One of the difficulties (and delights) of making programmes is the huge range of techniques producers are expected to master – everything from animation to zooming. But too much instruction too soon can overwhelm the beginner. To avoid this *On Camera – How to produce film and video*, has two parts. The first takes the reader step by step through basic production techniques. The second part, *Briefings*, deals subject by subject with things he or she will later want to know more about. Each chapter is rounded off with a summary.

The mythical San Totta Television Corporation sets the standard of incompetence which we can all strive to avoid. The Corporation was set up a few years ago by the government of the State of San Totta and quickly won a special place in the affections of those who watch it and those who work in it. Hence the nickname 'Totter TV' – a term of endearment which embraces agonies of frustration and abysses of boredom. Like Golden Turkey awards in the cinema, Totter is the small screen's badge of shame.

This book sets out guiding principles for each stage in making a programme, principles which hold good everywhere and are as valid for the private video or ciné enthusiast as they are for the professional. Pictures and sound take on a life of their own on the screen. The viewer judges them for what they are, not for where they came from. It doesn't matter if they reach the screen via a transmitter or cable or are replayed on a videocassette recorder. It doesn't even matter if they were shot on film or tape. What does matter is that they should have impact and tell the story the producer intends. The key to this is to know enough about the many disciplines connected with pictures and sound to be able to use them creatively. This is the key which this book seeks to provide.

NOTE:
Throughout the book it is assumed that the producer and director are the same person; a brief attempt to unravel their different functions has been made in the glossary at the end of the book. The pronoun 'he' should also be taken to refer to 'she' throughout the book: feminists must forgive me for failing to find a non-sexist substitute.

On Camera

Part One:

BASICS

BASICS

Ideas

Most how-to-do-it television guides start with a short lecture on the importance of ideas in programme-making. I will do so as well. But the truth is that San Totta TV manages quite well without ideas – instead its producers use formulas for their programmes.

formulas

Caesar Andante's 'Sport Round-up' takes a camera to a few convenient games each week. He then adds an introduction from the studio to each videotape and that's his slot filled for the week. Virginia Donna's women's programme has a slightly more ambitious formula: every week there's a song from a children's choir in the studio and the rest of the programme is filled with an interview or report about some meeting organised by the Women's Institute of San Totta. Light entertainment, religious, children's and chat (or interview) programmes all have their own formulas.

Nothing wrong with that: all formulas started off as ideas once – **good** ideas, or they wouldn't have developed into formulas. And formulas offer some useful advantages. Producers aren't exposed to the risk of failure – they know their programmes will work. Viewers know exactly what to expect from each programme and a few acquire the habit of viewing regularly. San TTV's General Manager, Magnus Vision, is happy too: his programmes have a safe following and nothing radical or unexpected is broadcast which might ruffle the conservative tastes of the government VIPs he has to get his funds from.

But in the long run formulas have a built-in element of failure, a sort of biodegradable element which guarantees that they will eventually rot away. Because in the long run formulas become tired and predictable and boring. You know that has happened when you can predict more than 50 per cent of a programme's contents before you've seen it.

The way to avoid this sorry end is to keep your formula fresh by always being on the lookout for ways to improve it. In countries with a long tradition of television you will be surprised how even programmes with a highly successful formula (like the news) have changed over the years – the result of new ideas introduced to keep an old and indispensable formula popular and alive.

But if you don't have a formula, you need an idea. So what in television is an idea?

To answer that, we first have to think about another question: what is television for? The usual answer to this question lists two objectives for programmes:

1   to entertain.
2   to inform.

For our purposes these are perfectly good objectives. They also provide a simple test for a programme idea. All you need do is ask yourself

1   does my idea entertain?
2   does my idea inform?

A 'yes' to question one is necessary for each and every programme idea without exception. All programmes must entertain the viewer in some way or quite simply there won't be any viewers, just people who have left their television on by mistake, or are waiting for the next programme. In fact the most useful definition for entertainment is 'something which people want to watch'. It needn't entertain only in the song-and-dance sense. It can interest, surprise, amuse, shock, stimulate or provoke the audience, but it must make them want to watch. That's entertainment.

People aren't paid to watch

16

A 'yes' to question two ('informing') is necessary for all programmes except those intended purely as entertainment (song-and-dance programmes, comedy, music programmes and so on). Informing means leaving the viewer at the end of the programme knowing a little more about something than he knew at the beginning.

If you have an idea which deserves a 'yes' to question two, you have a programme idea. But beware – your idea **must** also deserve a 'yes' to question one ('entertaining') if it's to be worth pursuing. What's the point of being informative if you're so unentertaining (so boring and predictable) that no one wants to watch? Reading the telephone directory on air, for example, could be called informative, but it's unlikely to be entertaining. Remember people aren't paid to watch television.

TV and information

Another point about being informative. Television is surprisingly bad at conveying detailed information to an audience. Newspapers, for example, can deliver far more information far faster. It would take about an hour to read four pages of a broadsheet paper out loud on television. Showing pictures other than that of the newsreader would slow things down even more. To make things worse, television viewers all have to receive their information at the same speed (this can delay the quick-witted unnecessarily and confuse the slow) and no one can go back to look again at the bits he didn't catch the first time round.

On the other hand the great advantage of television is that it can bring facts to life and present them in an entertaining way. But only a very limited number of facts in a given time. So you the producer have to be ruthless about deciding which are the most important facts and present only those in your programme. Doing this and being fair and balanced at the same time is one of the most difficult things a producer has to do. But it has to be done: programmes clogged with facts leave the viewer so bored and bewildered that in the end he leaves you.

thinking up ideas

So where are these entertaining and informative programme ideas going to come from? Thinking up ideas and ways of presenting them effectively is of course the most important and creative part of the producer's job – it's even more important than the procedures and techniques which this book contains. The idea behind the programme must be the master; technique must be the servant. That's the right order of priorities and you should always stick to it: never let production techniques dictate the content of your programme.

17

identifying ideas

Because thinking up ideas is the creative heart of the producer's job it's not something that I – or anyone else – can do for you. But I can offer you some hints on identifying ideas.

1 Is there something you want to say to the world? Do you have strong feelings about some subjects?

If you do, then you are one of those people who will have little trouble thinking of programme ideas. Obviously the things which make your blood boil are things which other people will also have strong opinions about and so you have the makings of a programme setting out the facts for everyone to consider. But don't let your strong feelings unbalance your sense of fairness; television is not a personal soapbox.

2 Think about what you are really interested in and the chances are that you will have a programme idea that will interest other human beings.

It's sometimes difficult to identify your own interests. (I know that personally, if anyone asks me what my hobbies are, my mind immediately goes blank.) The way to do it is to analyse your own behaviour. Which bit of the newspaper do you read first? (fashion? sport? news?) What sort of music do you listen to and who are your favourite performers? What were the subjects of the last few interesting conversations you had? (knitting? jet planes? pet animals?) Which books do you browse through in the bookshop? Which films and TV programmes on which subjects do you prefer? The answers to these questions will probably suggest some topics which you could do something with. These are the areas you should be combing for your programme ideas.

I recommend your own interests as the place to start looking because this is where you are most likely to find the subjects which interest other people. Most people are just like you (and me): they enjoy seeing programmes about all sorts of people (successful or unsuccessful, courageous or cowardly, amusing or gifted or bungling or . . . any adjective you care to name except boring); they enjoy programmes about animals and children and curiosities like eggs without yolks and extrasensory perception. They aren't immediately attracted by programmes about export statistics, energy gaps and computer languages because on the whole they don't understand these subjects. I am not saying that you should always go for the sensational or trivial and avoid important subjects like the last three. But making informative and entertaining programmes about subjects like the last three is infinitely more difficult than making informative and entertaining programmes about the other subjects I have mentioned. So give yourself a chance of making successful programmes by picking subjects which people will want to watch, particularly for your first few programmes.

3   It's unfortunately true that the time when you most desperately need an idea is always the time when you can't think of anything. Avoid this embarrassing state of mind by keeping an ideas file. In this file you should jot down possible subjects for programmes, the names of interesting books or people who might provide a topic, cuttings from newspapers and magazines and anything else which might come in useful. You'll soon find that the problem with the ideas file is keeping it in reasonable proportions. But never mind – with a bulging ideas file behind you, you'll be able to get through even your least inspired days without too much anguish.

Keep an Ideas File

Of course you aren't always given the luxury of choosing your own subjects for programmes. Often you'll be asked to do a programme about something which may not interest you and you won't be able to say no. But once you have accepted the assignment it's your job as producer to come up with an idea which will make the programme work. This happened once to Totta's current affairs producer, Eustace Sugar. He was asked to do a programme about the San Totta Army (SanTA for short) to celebrate Constitution Day. Eustace thought for a bit and made the following proposal: he would visit all three of the country's military bases with a camera crew and . . . .

Unfortunately there was no 'and'. That was as far as his idea went. Not a thought about what he was going to shoot when he got there. Was Eustace's programme idea a good one? Let's apply our two questions.

1   does it entertain?

Answer – no. Undoubtedly there are interesting things going on at the military bases but Eustace is unlikely to find them since he has no idea what he's looking for.

2   does it inform?

Again no. Eustace has no idea what he wants to tell his viewers about the army. So by setting out to tell them about everything he sees at the bases he ends up by swamping them with information and telling them nothing.

What Eustace needs is a bit of research to come up with a programme idea which is both entertaining and informative. Perhaps a look at how the army has developed in the last 10 years. Or a report on the way the military system can turn unsophisticated villagers into skilled handlers of complex modern weapons in a comparatively short time.

Now those are real programme ideas, Eustace. But to think of them – and certainly to turn them into programmes – you need to do some research. And that's the next step.

SUMMARY

Ideas

Keep formulas fresh by looking out all the time for new ways of improving them.

Test all new programme ideas by asking

1 does it entertain?   YES required for **all** ideas.

2 does it inform?   YES also required for all ideas (except purely entertainment programmes).

Television is not good at conveying large amounts of detailed information. So you have to select only the most important facts to put in your programme and leave the others out.

Hints for thinking up good ideas:

1 Do programmes about things you feel strongly about

2 Give yourself a chance of making successful programmes by picking subjects which interest human beings (the extraordinary interests people more than export statistics).

3 Keep an 'Ideas File'.

Research

Totta producers are not very keen on research.

In one way it seems rather inferior work, something for secretaries and very junior production assistants to do (there are no San TTV researchers). In another way it seems to be rather superior work, in fact something beyond the competence of programme-makers, something which government information officers or the clever chaps at the national museum provide ready-made and straight off the shelf.

As a result Totta programmes aren't researched at all. Eustace Sugar, as we know, makes a habit of turning up with his crew at a location and shooting whatever happens to be going on. Romeo Landmark, the sports commentator, rarely knows the name of more than three players in each team when he's commentating on a football match. He certainly has no facts and figures about the recent records of the two teams.

For more ambitious programmes (such as hour-long documentaries) Oscar Boney, the former school inspector turned producer, gets a local expert to write a summary of the topic he's chosen. The resulting document is called a 'script'. And, as Oscar says, who needs research if you have a script?

The answer is: everyone needs research. Even if there's a handy summary written by some expert.

There are two points to be remembered about research:

1 Every programme needs it.
2 Producers should do their own.

Fairly obvious points, but they are often ignored. As a producer you must obviously have some knowledge of the topic you are making a programme about. This doesn't mean that you need to know as much as or more than the expert. But you do need to know enough to be able to decide what to put into the programme and what to leave out. The choice of facts which you think worth including may not always be the same as the choice the expert would make, but provided that you can justify it intelligently, your choice will probably be the most effective one for television.

do your own research

It follows therefore that you should do your own research. Because as you find out more and more about the programme subject you are the only person who is looking out for the points which will come over most effectively on television. No one will be able to recognise these points better than you. Your outside experts certainly won't be able to; that's not their job. Government information officers know more about publicity than programme-making. The clever chaps at the national museum are more interested in collecting than selecting facts. And academics are always aiming at the definitive written (not televisual) account. When it comes to finding and selecting facts for television, you the producer are the expert.

think in pictures

You are also the only person who will be – or should be – thinking in pictures and sequences of pictures. An author working on a book finds his thoughts grouping themselves into paragraphs; a television producer should find his thoughts forming themselves into visual sequences. You have to look out for the good individual shot which sums up a situation, but you can't construct a good programme out of a succession of isolated shots, any more than you can write a good book by jotting down isolated facts. So always be on the lookout for situations which will yield not only pictures but sequences of pictures – these are the building blocks of your programme.

So how do you do research? The answer is – in any way possible. Read anything you can find on the subject. Telephone likely informants and go and talk to them personally if they sound interesting. Ask around to see if your friends and colleagues have useful contacts. Visit places and exhibitions. Look up references in the library. View previous programmes on the subject. Think, use your imagination and discuss your subject with anyone who will listen. Be open to new ideas – research should be an enjoyable, enlightening experience, not a desperate search for material to prop up your prejudices. Now is also the time to start thinking about music, if you intend using it in your programme. It could affect the way you handle your

Think in visual sequences

pictures. If you have a researcher, do the most important pieces of research together and split up for the rest, comparing notes afterwards.

using a tape-recorder   If you can lay hands on a tape-recorder, record any important conversations with people who might contribute to your programme. Make the recordings good enough to be edited and used over the relevant sequences in the finished programme; often you find that people are never again as fresh and interesting as the first time you meet them. But check that using a recording made like this does not violate any agreements made with the sound recordists' union. If it does, think about taking a sound recordist along for first meetings with key contributors to the programme, particularly if they are old or likely to be nervous (it would obviously be too expensive to have a sound recordist with you on all your research meetings).

Of course how you research depends on how much time you have. If you have any choice in the matter (and often you won't), give yourself enough time to become clear in your own mind what the programme will say and how it will say it. When you know that, then you've done most of your research.

keep a notebook   A final point – keep a notebook for each production. Put in it the facts and figures you have found out from your research, lists of the names and addresses of everyone involved in the programme, lists of possible sequences, notes of your expenses and so on. Read through it at intervals while you are doing your production: ideas which you rejected at an earlier stage may be worth reviving now that your programme has more shape to it. Re-reading a well-kept notebook can help bring order to that jumble of half-thought-out ideas swirling round inside your head. And when the production is finished, don't throw away the notebook. The contacts and ideas in it may be useful for another programme some day.

SUMMARY

Research

Every programme needs research.

As a producer you should do your own so that

1   you know enough about the subject to select the important points for television yourself and,

2   during research you will recognise the material which will come across best on television – no one else can do this for you or as well as you.

Think in pictures and sequences of pictures.

Follow up all likely leads.

Be open to new ideas.

Start thinking about your choice of music.

Record first conversations with likely contributors.

Keep a notebook.

Recce

Recce is short for reconnaissance, a word most often found on the lips of soldiers, who use it to describe the operation of going ahead of the main body of troops to spy out the land. Though of course, like television people, soldiers also usually say 'recce' instead of reconnaissance.

In television, as in war, a recce, though often impossible, is always advisable. Why?

There is no one major reason, just a host of minor ones.

Obviously if you have visited the location and have had a good look at what you intend to do, you are more likely to make economic and effective use of your time on location with the whole crew. Being well prepared always pays dividends – for both programmes and budget.

Other benefits flow from meeting the people you intend to tape or interview (oh, yes – you recce people as well). Talking with them about your plans gives everyone a chance to sort out their ideas in advance. On the day itself you will often find that a camera – like a gun – doesn't help clear thinking much.

The discussion on the recce also makes non-television people realise how much work goes into making a programme. Finished programmes flow so effortlessly from the TV set in the living room that most people assume that making the programme is also effortless. They envisage cameramen stepping from fast cars shooting from the hip, a quick chat followed by a short interview and that's it – the whole process as brief and bloodless as a well-organised bank raid. As a result they tend to allocate far too little time for their part of the programme.

Don't disillusion them too much – or they might withdraw their co-operation. But as you do your recce, the truth will slowly dawn on them that programme-making is more like working than robbing a bank.

So what do you do on a recce? The following checklist will be helpful.

1   *look around*
    Have a good look around the location and see what it has to offer.

25

2   *talk to people*
Talk to people there at length. Be curious about anything
and everything which promises something relevant for your
programme. Something they say or you notice may suggest a
new idea for – or way of – doing your story.

3   *check sun*
Check where the sun will be when you come back for your
videorecording or filming. This is important. A late
afternoon sun low on the horizon can make some scenes
impossible to shoot. A bright sun behind a building can cast
so black a shadow on its front that no film stock or videotape
will produce an acceptable picture.

4   *list sequences*
Make a list of the sequences you intend to film and discuss it
with the people there. Ask them to help with any
arrangements.

5   *list shots*
Work out a rough list of the shots you want for each
sequence. Try and think of some which are a bit unusual but
still fit into your story: perhaps a high shot from the top of
the camera car or a street-level shot with the cameraman
standing inside a ditch (preferably without water in it). An
unusual angle can often turn a commonplace scene into an
interesting shot. So ask to shoot from low roofs, high cranes,
conveyor belts and so on. Remember that as a television
producer you can frequently get permission to put your
camera in positions which would be forbidden to ordinary
members of the public (on the front of railway engines,
half-way up ships' masts, underground in mines and so on).
So use this advantage to the full; you're there on behalf of
your viewers. Look out in particular for the shot which 'says
it all' – the shot which in one unforgettable instant sums up
the nurse's devotion to her patient, the shot which captures
the fan club's enthusiasm for the footballer.

The most interesting shots are often to be found at the point
where things are changing: the first time the new machine is
switched on in the factory, the moment the air hostess tries
on her new uniform, the day the ship is towed off for
scrapping. Buildings are more interesting while they are
going up or coming down, schools when their pupils are
beginning or ending their break in the playground. On the
whole television is wasted presenting things which are static;
it is at its best when showing things which are happening or
changing before the viewer's eyes. You know you've found
that sort of shot or sequence when what the cameraman is
doing is not the most interesting happening on location.

Show things when they
are changing

6 *electricity*
Check that there is electricity for your lights and what sort of
plugs are in use. Check also on any high-powered electric,
radar, magnetic or X-ray devices in the vicinity which might
interfere with sound or videorecording. Modern industry
and the military seem to be using more and more of such
devices. They can create havoc, particularly for
videorecorders and radio mikes.

7 *sound*
Listen to the noises at the location. If they come from
sources which the viewer won't see in your shot they sound
louder when recorded than they really are and can be
extremely distracting. Continuous noise from places like the
building site next door, a busy road or an airport is probably
best dealt with by setting up a shot which incidentally shows
the source of the noise. Quiet sounds like air-conditioning
machines or aquarium pumps are best dealt with by asking if
they can be switched off while you shoot. Do this on the recce
to allow time for any special arrangements to be made.
Don't forget to ask the locals about flying times at the
helicopter training school just over the horizon, or the
factory full of circular saws which happens to be on
half-time working the day you do your recce. Its return to
full-time working on your shooting day may halve your
working time.

8 *shooting permission*
Double-check that you have permission to shoot from all the
people you need to ask. Does this include the police? Minor
officials like public relations officers are often reluctant to
admit that they aren't actually entitled to give permission.
You have to be tactful about finding out who is.

27

9 *fix shooting day*
Make sure your contacts know the day and time you intend
to come back for shooting, and what is expected of them on
the day. Check that market days, early closing or late
shopping days, school terms or holidays, high or low tides,
unexpected fairs, carnivals, festivals or sports events won't
interfere with your shooting.

10 *refreshments and parking*
Check that there is a place nearby where your crew can get
food and drink (and go to the toilet) if shooting will take
more than a short time. If in town make sure there will be no
parking problems. If out of town select an area where
parked cars will be out of shot.

11 *special equipment*
Make a note of any non-standard equipment you might
need: special mounts or lenses for the camera, light filters
for 'star' or diffusion effects, a clockwork camera for filming
in coalmines or on oil or gas tankers where there is a danger
that electrical sparks may set off an explosion. Walkie-
talkies are indispensable for almost any scene where the
camera is some distance from the action: for example, shots
of cars and boats travelling. Will the crew need wellington
boots, bathing costumes or other special clothing?

12 *take a stills camera*
It's often useful to take a stills camera with you on the recce.
A photograph can help the cameraman choose the right
lights for the interior you have in mind, or give the graphic
artist an idea for a style which will fit the programme
beautifully. Photographs are particularly useful if you are
doing a drama shot partly on location and partly in the
studio: the set designer, costume designer, props man and
studio lighting and sound supervisors will all find a good set
of photographs an enormous help.

13 *publicity stills*
Your stills camera will also remind you to look out for
possible publicity photographs for the programme. If you
see anything promising, make a note to arrange for a stills
photographer to come with you on the shooting day.

14 *how to get there*
Lastly, make sure that you can give clear and accurate
instructions on how to reach the location. A sketch map is
often useful. If the location is in the middle of nowhere it
may be a good idea to arrange to meet somewhere easy to
find and then travel in convoy. Or, alternatively, if there will
be a particularly large number of crew and participants, put

up cards with distinctive arrows and a code word at key road junctions. But don't mention TV or you may attract an unwanted crowd!

recceing programmed events

Occasionally you will be asked to tape or film an event which hasn't been arranged purely for your benefit and which you therefore won't be able to stop and start as you wish (presentation and opening ceremonies, graduation days and so on). When you recce these events you have to decide first which part of the proceedings you are interested in and then go on to find out in as much detail as possible what is actually going to happen in these sections. Often the organisers of the event won't have thought through all the details themselves, in which case you can tactfully become one of the organisers and help them arrange the proceedings as much as possible to your mutual benefit.

All this preparation can involve you in a great deal of work, particularly if you intend to record a large part or even all the events in the programme (rarely necessary unless you are doing an outside broadcast). But it's absolutely vital if your cameraman (or cameramen) are to avoid getting themselves into a terrible tangle because they don't know who does what next. The classic case was Vincent Toolate's coverage of a mixed old people's choir (Vincent is San TTV's news producer). The ladies were lined up on one side of the stage and the men on the other, with the solo singer in the front. The cameraman started on a wide shot and then when the men started singing he slowly zoomed in to cover them. Just before he finished the zoom they stopped singing and the ladies started. He wobbled for a moment, wondering whether to pan to the ladies, and decided against it. The ladies went on singing for a time so he then decided to pan to them. Just as he finished his pan, the ladies stopped singing and the men started. . . .

You can see that the possibilities for confusion are endless. A proper recce (preferably during a rehearsal for an event such as this) and Vincent could have avoided all the problems. If the cameraman could have accompanied him on the recce, so much the better. But that's a refinement which Totta hasn't thought of yet.

SUMMARY

Recce

Always advisable, not always possible.

Recce is part of the research. Use it to:

1   look around the location

2   talk to people there

3   check the position of sun

4   work out possible sequences

5   look out for interesting shots, particularly those which show things changing or 'say it all'

6   check the electricity supply and for high-power hazards for sound or video

7   check for noise problems both obvious and hidden

8   double-check shooting permissions

9   check contacts are clear about shooting times and dates. Check calendar, tide tables for possible shooting snags.

10 check crew feeding and toilet arrangements. Arrange car parking.

11 are walkie-talkies or special equipment for cameras or crew needed?

12 take photographs which might help studio-based technicians.

13 look for publicity photographs. If you think of any, make a note to arrange for a photographer to come on shooting day.

14 can you give clear 'how to get there' instructions?

Recce programmed events in great detail.

Take a cameraman on recces with you if possible.

Check the electricity supply

Options

San Totta TV is safe TV. Its producers stick to the techniques they know and avoid experiments. That way there's no chance of having a big failure with a programme. Unfortunately there's also no chance of having a big success.

So San TTV's viewers are restricted to a diet of talking heads and filmlets with muzak for sound tracks (synchronised sound effects are so rare that you could be forgiven for thinking that we were in the era of the silent movie). All programmes are fronted by presenters sitting in the same San TTV Presenter's Chair (viewers know it's the same one because they can recognise its squeak). And the continuity announcements are also the same every day; the printed script is simply changed for each day's schedule by putting in the appropriate programme titles. In fact Totta's producers have been sticking to the same techniques so faithfully since the station opened that they seem to have forgotten that there are other possibilities.

All producers should always try and broaden their personal range of production techniques. So here is a list of techniques, an inventory of options which any television producer might use. The list is not complete. What list of this type could be? New techniques are always being developed and some talented producers can successfully use techniques which other equally talented producers can't.

Of course not all the techniques which follow can be used in the same programme. But experiment a little if you think a particular technique would help what you are trying to say. You will be pleasantly surprised how much difference a bit of extra effort and imagination can make.

A

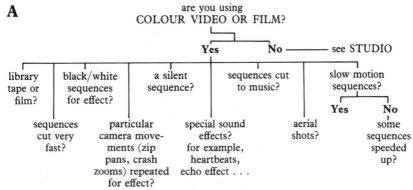

B

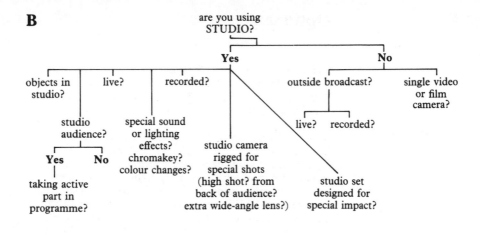

are you using
STUDIO?

Yes   No

objects in   live?   recorded?   outside broadcast?   single video
studio?   or film
                                                                           camera?

        studio   special sound   live?   recorded?
        audience?   or lighting
                            effects?   studio camera
Yes   No   chromakey?   rigged for
                            colour changes? special shots   studio set
taking active   (high shot? from   designed for
part in   back of audience?   special impact?
programme?   extra wide-angle lens?)

C

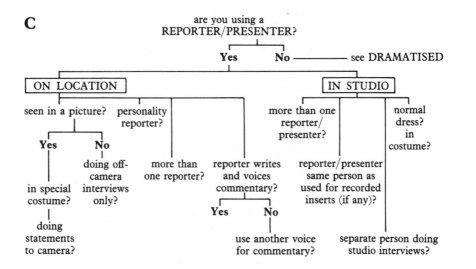

are you using a
REPORTER/PRESENTER?

Yes   No ——————— see DRAMATISED

ON LOCATION   IN STUDIO

seen in a picture?   personality   more than one   normal
                      reporter?   reporter/   dress?
Yes   No   presenter?   in
                      doing off-   costume?
                      camera   more than   reporter writes
in special   interviews   one reporter? and voices   reporter/presenter
costume?   only?   commentary?   same person as
                                                               used for recorded
doing   Yes   No   inserts (if any)?
statements
to camera?   use another voice   separate person doing
                                           for commentary?   studio interviews?

D is your programme
DRAMATISED?

on film or portable video?

in studio

actors
one person doing all parts solo?
several actors?
children playing some/all parts?

script
specially written?
partly improvised?
historical words re-enacted?

music?
song?
dance?

location
improved with constructed sets, props, lights?
or non-naturalistic abstract set –
for example, a cave or against the sky or on mountain?

other possibilities
puppets?
cartoons?
models?
shadows?

costume
historical?
formal?
casual?

archive or undramatised sequences mixed with dramatised?

E are you using
GRAPHICS?

maps?
diagrams?
graphs?
drawings?
animated?

captions
with special lettering?
drawn in shot?
written in unusual medium, for example, sand?
written with unusual material, for example, uncooked rice?
typed on screen?

paintings
specially done?
historic?

cartoons?

stills
specially shot?
from archive, newspapers, magazines, private collections?

recorded with camera movements?
cut to music?
with sound effects?

press cuttings
taped or filmed with camera movements?
key sentences typed out specially?
superimposed against video, film or still photo background?

When you watch television or films make a habit of noticing the techniques used. You might be able to use some of them (suitably adapted) in your own programmes. Remember that the director or producer whose work you are watching faced the same problems you are up against – did he always go for the easiest solution? I have just watched a film in which one scene shows a boy taking his first ride on a wild black stallion he has befriended. The first time the boy actually manages to get onto the stallion's back, boy and horse are swimming in the sea. The director chose to film the whole scene from under water so that all we see are the boy's legs carefully getting astride the horse. An imaginative, original idea which works beautifully.

Simpler ideas used with imagination and originality can come off just as well – try very hard to get some into your programmes. But always make sure the technique you choose helps to communicate the point you want to make. Techniques which aren't quite right can easily get in the way of your message instead of putting it over.

SUMMARY

Options

Television offers a vast range of techniques for getting the message across to the audience, many of them very simple to use. Don't always go for the obvious – see if there is a better, more imaginative technique for communicating what you want to say.

Enlarge your own armoury of techniques by watching how other directors handle their material. You could adapt some of their ideas for your own programmes.

Techniques should complement, not confuse the message you are trying to get across.

Treatment

The preliminary research is now finished. It may have lasted a month, a week or the time it takes to make a telephone call. But at the very least you will have thought things over, asked a few questions, got some answers and worked out a way of doing your programme.

Now you are ready to do the treatment. This consists of writing down on a piece of paper all the things you intend to put into the programme. In note form, with the visuals on the left and an indication of what the sound will be on the right. Something like this:

Opening of new Bridge over Rigwe River

	picture	sound
1	crowds arrive for opening ceremony	commentary: new bridge opening today – bridge replacing ferry
2	ferry on last trip	ferry working since 1936 – last trip on Sunday at noon
3	interview ferry captain c/a* photo of rowing skiff	sync:'end of an era – ferry replaced rowing skiffs – early hostility to ferry – sad to be going'
4	library film: new bridge being built	commentary: new bridge started two years ago (use original commentary)
5	interview consultant engineer	sync:'difficulties building bridge . . .'
6	crowd assembled for opening	vox pop**: what difference will new bridge make to everyday life?

7	arrival of VIPs and opening ceremony	sync, and commentary on events as needed
8	celebrations	ditto
	(*c/a: cutaway shot)	(** see glossary)

This is probably as much detail as you need in your treatment. But why bother doing a treatment at all?

The advantages will emerge as you do it. Putting down on paper what you intend to do concentrates the mind wonderfully. For example:

– will your ideas work?

– have you planned enough sequences for the story you want to tell?

– do the planned sequences add up to what is needed in both time and content?

– have you left anything out?

All this – and more – will emerge as you do your treatment.

With experience you will be able to recognise the strong and weak points in your story, and this knowledge will serve you well when you come to shooting it. You don't have to stick slavishly to every sequence you've planned. While you are shooting, new facts may emerge (the process of finding out things never stops); or some events you had high hopes for may turn out to be disappointing. If this happens there is nothing to stop you changing your planned sequence. But having a workable treatment on paper doubles your chance of producing a good programme.

Totta producers of course avoid doing a treatment at all costs. Virginia Donna finds that if she does a treatment for the items in her weekly women's magazine programme it looks a bit bare . . . as indeed her programme is, since it never departs from its very basic formula.

Eustace Sugar doesn't like putting his ideas down on paper; he finds he can't think of anything to put down. He once did a programme about San Video traffic jams which consisted of 25 minutes of – you guessed it – traffic jams. And nothing else. The treatment for this programme (if there had been one) would have read 'shots of traffic jams'. Even Eustace would have realised that there was something wrong with this as a programme idea!

Some events may be
disappointing

estimating duration

How long will the programme be if you do all the sequences
you have in your treatment? Estimating this can be a
problem. Have you planned enough, or too much?

The trick here is to estimate the likely length of each
sequence individually and then add up the estimates to
arrive at a total. You will find it helps if the list of points you
want to make in the sound column of your treatment is as
complete as possible. If you allow 15 seconds for each point
plus something for pictures without commentary your total
won't be very far out. Let's see how this works with the
Rigwe River programme.

Sequence 1
crowds arrive for opening   commentary: new bridge
ceremony   opening today – bridge
                                   replacing ferry

DURATION ESTIMATE: two points, about 15 secs
each = 30 secs. Allow extra 5 secs for opening of
programme (commentary can't begin immediately
programme does!). But don't bother with odd seconds too
much. So call total for sequence ½ **min**.

Sequence 2
ferry on last trip   ferry working since 1936 –
                                   last trip on Sunday at noon

DURATION ESTIMATE: two points, about 15 secs
each = 30 secs. Allow extra for film of ferry's last trip:
arriving, tying up at quay, blowing whistle and so on:
30 secs. Total, say **1 min**.

Sequence 3

interview ferry captain	'end of era – ferry replaced rowing skiffs – early hostility to ferry – sad to be going'

DURATION ESTIMATE: 4 points, about 15 secs each = 1 min.
Allow extra time for captain talking round subject, say
30 secs. Total, say **1½ mins** (note c/a photo of rowing skiff
is to be used over sound of captain talking. So no extra time
allowance is needed).

Sequence 4

library film: new bridge being built	commentary: new bridge started two years ago (use original commentary)

DURATION ESTIMATE: the library film is particularly
interesting as it says the bridge will take only six months to
build! Allow time to introduce the library film (15 secs) plus
15 secs to make your commentary point (new bridge started
two years ago) plus 1½ mins for the original commentary on
the library film. Total, **2 mins**.

Sequence 5

interview consulting engineer	'difficulties building bridge'

DURATION ESTIMATE: 1 point = 15 secs. But obviously the
engineer will want to give details of his difficulties and his
talk is bound to ramble a little. So allow **1½ mins**.

Sequence 6

crowd assembled for opening	vox pop: what difference will new bridge make to everyday life?

DURATION ESTIMATE: allow 15 secs to set up the question for
the vox pop (a technique in which you ask lots of people the
same question one by one and then use short extracts from
their answers without repeating the question or introducing
their names*); then about 15 secs for each of six answers.
Total 1 min 45 secs. Call it **2 mins** for ease of calculation.

*For more about vox
pops see Briefing No. 9   And so on.

38

The advantage of making your estimates sequence by sequence is that your overestimates and underestimates will tend to cancel out, leaving you with a fairly accurate idea of the length of the completed programme. But just to be on the safe side always make sure your planned sequences add up to about 25% more than you need. It's much easier to cut things out of programmes than to put them in. Indeed programmes usually benefit from being planned a little overlong and then shortened.

how many shooting days?

How long will the programme take to shoot? The treatment makes this easy to calculate. The Rigwe bridge story is obviously going to take the best part of a day: a couple of hours to cover events connected with the ceremony and another couple of hours for the interviews with the captain and the engineer. For a programme involving several locations work out the shooting days required by allocating days or half days for each location. Don't forget to allow for travel time.

Besides the help with planning and timing a story, doing the treatment yields a further bonus: it gives you a chance to sit back for a moment and take stock of the way the programme is going. Has the research uncovered enough of the right sort of contributors and facts? Are there enough sequences and pictures to make the story come alive for television? Is your programme idea still entertaining and informative now you know more about it? This is the time to go back to the test questions in the first chapter and reapply them to your project.

identifying your story

You may sometimes have difficulty doing a treatment along the lines I have suggested. Often this difficulty is in itself a sign that you have not thought things through clearly. Is your story strong enough? What is it trying to say? You may find that you have so many disorganised facts in your mind that you can't decide what the story is or how you should tell it. If this is your problem, it can be a great help to turn to a friend and tell him or her in about twenty simple everyday words what your programme is about (just as if your friend had asked). For example: 'I'm showing the opening of the new bridge and looking at how people used to cross the Rigwe River before.' The very effort of putting your story in a few simple words tells you a) if you have a story, b) what your story is, and c) if it's entertaining and informative. Your brain will do it almost automatically if you let it, as long as you stick to simple spoken language. Often it's the pompous phrases (like 'Rigwe River Overbridge Construction Project – Final Phase') which obstruct your understanding of what the story is about. Then once you have identified your story you can organise your material to put it across in the most effective way.

Beware if the summary of your story is something vague like 'this film shows the work of the police' or 'this film shows the things that go on in our military bases' (this was Eustace Sugar's story). Such stories suggest no reason why any viewer should watch; they promise nothing informative or interesting. If instead you say: 'I want to show the new techniques the police are using to cope with the rising crime rate', you have identified a specific story which is likely to yield something worth watching.

Another useful tip for finding your story is to ask yourself 'Why am I doing this story now? Could it be done next year or could it have been done last year?' Thinking about these questions forces you to pinpoint the relevance of your story to the viewer. Perhaps the best way of appreciating the importance of defining precisely what you are trying to say is to consider that fast disappearing breed of film, the travelogue. Because the problem with the travelogue is that it has no story; it has nothing to say about the places it shows you. As a result the viewer is condemned to watch an endless succession of folk dances and postcard pictures. Travelogue commentaries have become things to mock: 'Take a ride into history on a gentle gondola'; and, 'Nowhere is the age-old culture of these nature-loving folk more clearly seen than in this traditional dance of the cheeses'; and 'So we say farewell to this land blessed with music and laughter'.

No wonder the travelogue is dying on its feet. Make sure that your programmes don't by being absolutely clear about what you want to say.

SUMMARY

Treatment

When preliminary research is over, do a treatment. Put the picture on the left, sound on the right.

Check your treatment to see if you have

– a workable programme idea

– enough material to cover the story at the length you want

– left anything out.

Estimate the total duration by estimating the duration of each sequence in turn and adding them up.

For safety plan about 25% more material than you think you will have time for.

Work out the shooting days needed.

Define the story by summing it up in about 20 simple words.

Is it entertaining and informative?

How relevant is it to the average viewer – why should he or she watch it?

Why are you doing this story now and not at some other time?

Location Shooting

Totta's documentary producer, Oscar Boney, never goes on location with the crew when the time comes to shoot his programme. Quite unofficially, of course. 'Well,' he reasons to himself, 'I don't really know what I want to shoot anyway and perhaps the cameraman can sort out something good. After all, he's had more experience on location than I have. Anyway I'm much too busy to go out now. I've got to fill out my car allowance claim and . . . .'

At least Oscar scores two out of three for his reasons. He isn't sure what he wants to shoot (very little research, no recce probably, certainly no treatment) and the cameraman almost certainly has more experience of location shooting than he does. Though you would have to cut off his allowances before he admitted it in public.

It's fairly obvious what the drawbacks of this stay-at-home policy are. True – Oscar's absence may have no noticeable effect on any individual shot. But the overall coverage will almost certainly suffer (people who can successfully direct and operate the camera at the same time are very rare indeed – there's simply too much for one person to do). The one person who is certain to suffer is of course Oscar, because if he doesn't go out on location with his crew he misses the shooting experience he could be acquiring and has no chance of improving his personal expertise. So he manages at one stroke to deprive himself of two chances: the chance of making a good programme now (if it is good, it won't be because of him), and the chance of making better ones in the future. Because, believe me, there's no teacher like experience.

So what do you, as a fairly new producer, do with an experienced cameraman (or camerawoman) on location?

brief the cameraman First of all explain to him briefly what the programme is about and show him the relevant part of the treatment. Don't be discouraged if he doesn't want to know about the programme and doesn't want to read the treatment; some cameramen like to work on a shot-by-shot basis and ignore everything else. If you meet this sort of cameraman, very briefly tell him what the story is anyway; there's always a chance he might become interested.

Then start shooting the most important bits of the story first. That way if the equipment fails or the weather worsens

Do exteriors before the
weather changes

you have at least recorded something. In fact as modern
technology is becoming more and more reliable, the weather
is likely to be the greater hazard. So as a rule it's a good idea
to do your exteriors first if the weather is right rather than
run the risk of it changing for the worse.

master shots

Start shooting each sequence by covering the main action all
the way through with a wide shot: this is often called the
'master' shot. Then get your contributors to repeat the
action (if necessary more than once) so that you can get the
close-ups and reaction shots you need. If you find it difficult

your mental TV

at first to break down the action into individual shots, close
your eyes and imagine a television set showing the sequence
you want to shoot. Watch the sequence, remember each

*Briefing No. 1 'The
Right Words '
explains the language of
shots and camera
movement.

picture (whether it's in close-up, medium shot or long shot,
how the camera moves and so on*) and there you have your
breakdown of individual shots. If you forget one of the shots
you can always rerun the sequence on your mental TV.

shooting order

You don't have to do the shots in the order in which they
will appear in the finished story (though jumping around
unnecessarily can complicate matters and lead to continuity
problems). But you should try and avoid taking the camera
back to a position once you have left it – that's an obvious
waste of time. The way to avoid this is to sort out in advance
all the shots you need with the camera in one position (all the
shots in one 'set-up') and then shoot them one after another.
Then you move to your next set-up and shoot there. This is
not only a logical way to proceed but can also have other
benefits.

poison-in-the-pop-bottle story

Suppose, for example, that you are doing a story pointing out that many shops are breaking the law by selling dangerous poisons like weedkiller in old soft-drink bottles and are not even bothering to label the bottles clearly. If in your story your reporter has to go into a shop to buy some bottles of poison and then has to come out of the shop with his bottles and make a statement to camera, it is obviously more economical and less trouble to do all the exterior shots first. Then you go into the shop and shoot your reporter buying the bottles and interviewing the shopkeeper.

You will notice that even with a short story like this there are at least two ways of putting the sequence together for the finished programme.

either	*or*
ext. shop	ext. shop
reporter enters shop	reporter enters shop
buys poison	buys poison
comes out of shop	interviews shopkeeper
statement to camera	leaves shop
interviews shopkeeper.	statement to camera.

The crucial point is where do you put the interview with the shopkeeper when you are assembling your story? You should have decided this when you did your treatment as the position of the interview in the final assembly will make a big difference to the emphasis of the story. The thought may also have occurred to you at the treatment stage that the position of the interview depends on what the shopkeeper says (which in turn depends to some extent on what you ask him). Will he become angry when you ask him why he is selling a poisonous substance in bottles in which it could be mistaken for a soft drink? Or will he simply shrug his shoulders and say that all the shopkeepers do it?

If he becomes very angry, he may prevent your reporter doing his statement in front of the shop after the interview – that's a good reason for filming the statement before the interview. That way, you know you are safe – you have already recorded the statement. And of course if the shopkeeper stays cool during the interview, there's nothing to stop you doing another version of the statement after the interview, one that takes into account what the shopkeeper said. If you do that, you have given yourself a choice of ways in which to cut the story. And that usually means you have a chance of producing a better story – one choice **must** be better than the other. If you do only one version of the statement in this particular story there's no way of making sure you chose the better one.

You should now be able to see the advantages of thinking about the order in which to shoot even such an apparently straightforward story. The first advantage is that your planning has stopped you falling into the trap of leaving the statement to camera till after the interview – the shopkeeper might have stopped you if he had become angry, or it might have started to rain – and if one of these had happened, you may have had to return to your office with a half-covered story and an unnecessarily complicated editing problem.

And the bonus your planning has given you is the possibility of shooting a second version of the statement to camera, tailoring it to fit the interview more precisely and thus strengthening your story. It's worth doing your homework!

shooting ratios   How much should you shoot?

If you are using videotape you are probably under great pressure to have your story ready for transmission the same day; the great advantage of video is after all its immediacy. So how much you record is limited by two sorts of time: the time available before you have to transmit your story and the time available on the video editing machines. You will probably be short of both and so will be wise to limit your use of tape to what is needed to cover the story adequately. Remember editing video normally takes **at least** two and a bit times the time you have on tape: once to view it, once to find and transfer it, and a bit (how much depends on you) to make your editing decisions.

Totta TV still uses film for most of its documentary and current affairs programmes. So Totta film producers are not under as much pressure as those working with video; San TTV accepts that where film is concerned shooting, editing and transmission on the same day are normally possible only for the briefest news items.

As a result Totta producers are a little more free to choose how much film they use for each story. But this freedom is not something they always use wisely.

Their lady producer, Virginia Donna, for example, is an enthusiastic economiser of film and always aims for a 1 to 1 shooting ratio (in other words, every foot she shoots, she shows). Virginia would disapprove very strongly of the suggestion of shooting an alternative statement to camera in the poison-in-the-pop-bottles story. 'A waste of film,' she would call it.

How much you shoot depends to some extent on how good you want your story to be. For the poison-in-the-pop-bottles film you need at the very least a 2 to 1 ratio (2 feet shot for every one used in the finished story); a 3 to 1 ratio would be better. You must provide the film editor with enough to give him a chance of cutting together something good. Longer documentaries need at least 5 to 1. Up to 10 to 1 is acceptable. Filming ratios used to be much, much higher when film stock and processing costs were a lot cheaper. But don't run away with the idea that exposing film will **in itself** give you a better story. Oscar Boney once turned in a ratio of 25 to 1 and no one at Totta knew how to edit this mountain of rushes into a transmittable film. What you shoot is as important as how much.

To make a successful programme you have to pull off a difficult trick: you have to pay an enormous amount of attention to every detail in every shot and yet at the same time you must never lose sight of the overall shape of the programme. Here are some points to bear in mind:

Homework
Do your homework thoroughly (research, recce, treatment, etc).

Every shot is important
Shoot every shot as if it were the most important in the programme – after all, while it is on the screen it **will** be the most important shot in the programme.

The GV or Establisher
For each location or building in which you are shooting do at least one exterior GV (General View) or 'establisher', even if you don't think you'll need it. You'll be surprised how often this shot will get you out of trouble when you come to editing.

The Introductory Shot for Interviewees
For each person whom you interview you should do at least one shot showing the person doing something other than being interviewed by your reporter. You don't necessarily have to use the shot in the finished programme but it's sensible to have one available if needed. If you can show your interviewee doing something which gives the viewer an insight into the sort of person he is (gardening or running up the stairs or exercising the dog), so much the better. The important things to remember are that this introductory shot should have a background different from the

background for the interview and that your interviewee should go out of the picture at the end of the shot. If this doesn't happen you will have introduced a 'jump' cut between your introductory shot and your interview shot and you may find you can't use your introductory shot in the programme.

Avoid Jump Cuts

You are in the editing room, you have a shot of a man running down the street and as he comes near the camera you cut straight to a shot of him sitting in his armchair reading the newspaper. You have just put a jump cut into your programme: the man has 'jumped' instantly between two locations and the effect is not pleasing to the viewer. The way to avoid this is to let travelling subjects such as people, cars, aeroplanes and so on leave the picture before you stop shooting; in the example above you should carry on shooting till the man has run past the camera. Or you could cut to a close-up of the man's drink next to the armchair before showing him sitting there. As long as there is some picture **without** the man between the shots of the man in the two locations you won't need to worry about a jump cut.

You should always plan your shooting to avoid jump cuts; shortening shots in the cutting room will give you more than enough jumps to worry about anyway. Ways of getting round these are discussed in what follows and in the chapter on editing.

The nuisance jump cut: editing an unwanted section of dialogue between 'lovely' and 'clean' has made the speakers jump down the platform

Cutaways

There are two sorts of jump cuts – one of them is a big nuisance and one of them is the price we have to pay for television's marvellous ability to telescope time. You need cutaways to get over both sorts of jump cut – if you can't avoid them any other way.

Steam engines have such lovely.... clean lines

47

the nuisance jump cut

Let's deal with the nuisance jump cut first. You want to take a section out of the middle of a piece of continuous action. It's fairly easy to shorten the sound without the viewer noticing that anything is missing. It isn't so easy with the picture – there is an obvious jump when the two shots at either end of the section you have removed are put next to each other. To cover this jump you have to cut away to something else (hence the term 'cutaway').

The most common situation where you come across the nuisance jump cut is in interviews; this is dealt with in detail in the following chapter. Here I just want to make the point that no one has come up yet with a totally satisfactory way of dealing with this sort of jump cut: virtually all the solutions are make-shift. That's why this sort of jump cut is a nuisance – because there is no visual, dramatic or logical reason for you to take the viewer's attention away from the main action at this point. Your distracting cutaway is there for a purely technical reason, and that's not good. Remember, technique should be the servant not the master.

short-cutting time

The other sort of cutaway is much easier to do because it springs naturally from television's marvellous ability to short-cut the passing of time. Suppose you are shooting a funeral procession moving slowly down the road to the cemetery. You can hold the shot of the approaching procession for a fairly long time (even longer if you have some suitable music on the sound track). But long before the procession turns into the cemetery gates the viewer's interest in the shot will have dwindled. What is more natural than to cut away from the approaching procession to one or more shots of mourners weeping and then cut back to the procession turning into the cemetery gates? Notice that the cutaway(s) of the mourners need be on the screen only a fraction of the time that it really takes the procession to reach the cemetery gates and it will still look right to the viewer – that's what I mean by television's 'ability to short-cut the passing of time'.

When shooting you'll frequently find yourself wanting to short-cut the time it really takes to do things like getting into a car and driving away, cooking a meal, painting a picture or checking through a document. You can often get over the jump in time by covering the beginning and end of the action from different angles or with different size shots. The person leaving in his car, for example: start on a wide shot of the person getting in and then short-cut the time spent fumbling for the right key, fastening the seatbelt, starting the engine and so on by cutting to a low angle shot of the car moving off past the camera. But more often than not you need cutaways: people's faces and details of the main action; perhaps shots from the point of view of the main object in the sequence (in the funeral example perhaps a view of the spectators along the route as seen by someone in the procession). Make your cutaways contribute as much as possible to the content of your programme. Above all don't forget to do them – you are going to need them.

'Wallpaper' Shots

Your exterior GVs and your introductory shots for interviewees are both examples of 'wallpaper' shots. You need wallpaper shots like these to give the viewer something to look at while the commentary is talking about things which can't be illustrated directly. Shots of people driving or walking, landscapes and townscapes, traffic shots and GVs of children playing all make acceptable wallpaper.

Your treatment will tell you roughly how much you need; make sure you shoot enough. But beware if half or more of your shots are wallpaper: viewers want to see things happen on their screens. Of course the more relevant the wallpaper is to your story, the more acceptable it is.

'Insert' Shots

The finger on the switch, the dial on the machine, the bullet-hole through the window: these are some of the things which you may want to draw attention to in your programme and don't stand out well enough in the wide shots. So do close-ups of them, repeating the complete action (the finger comes into shot, flicks the switch, goes out of shot) to give the editor maximum freedom to choose the best possible cutting points for the insert. Remember any action you shoot in close-up should be done slightly slower than normal. Fast, jerky actions go in and out of the close-up frame so quickly that they can look comic.

Three for the Price of One

Here's a way of getting three shots for the price of one. Whenever you do a zoom ask the cameraman to hold the shot at the beginning of the zoom for about eight seconds and also the shot at the end of the zoom for about eight seconds. That way you have a choice of three shots to use in the editing room and it's only taken up an extra 20 seconds of your filming time (4 secs to ask the cameraman and 8 secs for each hold). It also gives you the chance of dropping the zooming part of the shot during editing and just using the two holds. Too many zooms can spoil a film, especially if there is no good reason for them. You should in particular avoid the ugly 'yo-yo' effect you get when you zoom in and then out again on the same shot.

Don't rely on Library Film

Cameramen who are in a hurry on location will sometimes say to you: 'You don't need to wait around for the shots you want of a police car (or ambulance) (or the National Assembly Building) because there are hundreds of shots in the library – I know, because I shot some myself only last week.'

Don't be misled. First of all the material that was shot last week never quite says exactly what you want your shot to say. The cameraman is also unlikely to know if the shot wasn't thrown away with the rest of the surplus shots after editing. If it does exist, it will probably take you ages to find it. And if you do manage to find it and by some fluke it's exactly what you want (most unlikely), it'll be third or fourth generation (if it's video) or scratched from all the handling it has had (if it's film). Either way it is likely to be less than top quality. Don't be fooled. Library material is good for shots which openly acknowledge their age (the deterioration in the quality almost enhances their effect); it can rarely be passed off as new specially-shot material. If you are at the right location and can see what you want, shoot it now. Sorry, Mr Cameraman.

Overlaps

Don't forget your overlaps – for both sound and vision.

In the poison-in-the-pop-bottles story, for example, when you were shooting the reporter entering the shop you should have continued the shot until well after he had gone through the door and was no longer visible from outside. Then when you were shooting his coming through the door with your camera inside the shop you should have started with a shot of the empty door with no reporter there. You then cue him to walk into shot and through the door. So in effect you have two shots and two sound recordings of him walking through the door – one from outside and one from inside. This overlap gives the editor and you a chance to choose the best point to cut from one shot to the other.

Crossing the Line

The best way to avoid 'crossing the line' is to use your mental TV. If two people are talking to each other, they normally look at each other. So if one is looking towards the right in one shot, the other should be looking towards the left in the next shot. If you see a car travelling towards the right of the screen on your mental TV and it goes out on the right, it must come in from the left in the next shot (or it will have appeared to change direction). If a golfer hits the ball out of the left side of one shot, you have to arrange matters so that the ball comes in from the right side in the next shot, or the two shots when cut together will look ridiculous.

As long as you keep checking your mental TV to see how your shots will look when cut together, you are unlikely to make the mistake of crossing the line. This is a much more reliable method than worrying about 'optical barriers' or which cheek is closer to the camera in interviews.

See also the buffer shot illustration on p. 121

In theory to avoid crossing the line you have to keep your camera on the same side of the action in successive shots (in front of the subject and interviewer when doing interviews, on the same side of the road when shooting the car). But the problem rapidly becomes more complicated. If you shoot a man and a woman walking right to left and talking to each other and the man is furthest away from the camera, a shot of the woman from his point of view will reverse the direction in which they appear to be walking. In this situation the need to have one speaker facing right and the other one left conflicts with the need to keep them walking in the same direction. The way round the problem is to avoid his point of view. Stick to shots from one side of the path they are treading and vary the angle if you need to by taking shots from directly in front or behind. The important thing is to keep your couple walking right to left.

If you are shooting four people sitting round a dinner table or playing cards, the crossing-the-line problem becomes very tricky. Here the direction people should face in successive shots depends on whose point of view the camera is adopting. As long as you don't keep changing the point of view and recognise the fact that each change involves rethinking some of the directions people face, then your

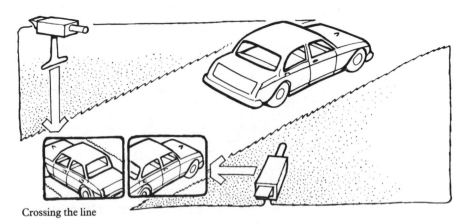

Crossing the line

mental TV and careful step-by-step analysis should resolve the difficulties without too much trouble.

Finally, don't get too obsessed with not crossing the line. The convention is broken in nearly every pop concert you see on screen with singers facing first left and then right in successive shots. By all means avoid crossing the line wherever possible by comparing the shots you will get from different camera positions on your mental TV. But keep things in proportion – crossing the line is at worst an irritant for your viewers. It's not – as some would have us believe – an offence deserving capital punishment.

Sound
The person who is forgotten most often on location is the sound recordist. .He or she needs to know the shot you have in mind just as much as the cameraman. So make a habit of telling the sound recordist what you are up to immediately after discussing the shot with the cameraman. You may have to change a shot slightly to help the recordist get over his problems; it's obviously useful to find this out as early as possible.

shoot sync

Shoot everything you can synchronised – it doesn't cost extra! And insist on using a clapper-board for all your shots; it's the simplest and most reliable system for identifying shots (and synchronising them with the right sound if you are using film). Even for video, '21 take 2' is a more memorable way of tagging a shot than the eight-digit time-code number. Now that most videorecorders offer a 'search' facility (fast forward spooling without losing the picture) it's much easier to find shots quickly if you use a clapperboard.

One of the most persistent sound problems on location is the noise which comes from a source not seen in the shot. Your brain automatically filters these sounds from your consciousness when you are concentrating on the picture (unless the noises are very loud) but the sound recording equipment picks them all up and makes them sound louder. Even a quiet hum from something like a refrigerator can be very irritating. Many of these noises can be stopped temporarily. Switch off the refrigerator just before you start shooting; you can often deal with radios and other machinery in the same way. Workmen using pneumatic drills (they always seem to turn up near locations) can usually be persuaded to down tools for a few moments with a little money. Take telephones off the hook before starting to shoot; they have a habit of ringing at awkward moments. You'll have to stop shooting while the inevitable jet aircraft passes overhead. If you can't get rid of off-camera sound, you may have to find a quieter location if you are trying to shoot something like a long interview. Or alternatively make sure the source of the sounds is seen in at least one shot in the sequence; after all, people would expect an interview in a busy market to be fairly noisy.*

*More about Sound in Briefing No. 6

Lighting

The other thing you have to keep an eye on during shooting is lighting. Setting up lights can be a very time-consuming business. So try and arrange the fewest possible set-ups which need lighting.

Leave the cameraman to look after the technical side; your job is to decide what you want. You should be asking yourself not just 'Is there enough light here for this shot?' but also 'How can I use the available light or the lights we have brought with us to improve this shot?' It's a mistake to think of lighting as just a technical requirement for recording pictures – it should contribute creatively as well as technically.

Make sure the lighting draws attention to the main object you want to see in the picture. You don't have to light every single corner of the background as brilliantly as if it was in an exhibition; lighting just isn't as evenly spread as this in real life. And those interesting areas of shadow which you would find in real life have the advantage of not distracting the viewer's attention from the main object.

Some cameramen will just put every available light on a scene unless they are given specific preferences by the director. So the best thing for you to do is to try to say what lighting you have in mind for each shot. For example: 'I'd like this scene brightly lit with not too many hard shadows, please' or 'Could you light the face gently to show those interesting lines and also keep the light on the wall behind rather low so as not to distract attention from the face'.

Thoughtful cameramen will also avoid double shadows from the nose and get rid of the big black shadow which so often falls on the wall behind an interviewee by moving him or her away from the wall.

The way to check lighting is to look at the scene through half-closed eyes. The more brightly lit things will then stand out in the picture: areas where there is a little less light will appear quite dark. If the things which become more prominent through half-closed eyes are the things you want to emphasise in your shot, all well and good. If they aren't, discuss possible changes with the cameraman.

Finally, be specially careful when you are doing a shot containing both very bright and very dark patches. The television system finds this strong contrast between light and dark very difficult to cope with even though your eyes may have no problem. Try and film against backgrounds where the light is more even if you possibly can.*

*More about Lighting in Briefing No. 5

Special points for video
Is shooting video different from shooting film?
The answer is: hardly at all.

For a start, all the points made in this chapter so far apply to video just as much as to film. Jump cuts, wallpaper, inserts, crossing the line and so on are all to do with pictures, not with the machinery for recording pictures. You wouldn't expect a programme to look different if it reached your screen via cable instead of being broadcast. Why should video or film make a difference? It's worth remembering that virtually none of your viewers will be able to tell anyway which medium you used on location.

don't shoot too much

That said, video does offer you certain advantages on location. The first one is the comparative cheapness of videotape compared to film. This gives you a little more freedom in how much you shoot. But beware. If you think that taping more means you need plan less, you'll end up with poorer material than you ought. Plan each shot and sequence as carefully for video as you would for film. The finished product will benefit and you will avoid the tedium of spending hours and hours of editing time looking through stacks of sloppily recorded tapes for the shots you need to tell your story.

run-up time for video

The only tape you should consciously 'waste' is the few seconds run-up at the start of each shot. Your editing machines need this to get into step with each other and thus give you a stable edit without the picture flickering. The time needed to get into step varies with the design of the machine but if you allow 10 seconds to run up, then you should have no problems. Of course if you have simply stopped the recorder with the 'pause' button on location, you don't need the run-up time. But using the pause button is not recommended for any but the briefest interruptions during shooting as it wears the videotape unnecessarily at one spot.

using the monitor

The other great advantage of video is its immediacy. On the whole this is not something you should exploit too much while actually on location. Playing back each shot immediately you have recorded it wears out batteries and wastes precious shooting time. Far better to take a monitor on location and check while you are lining up each shot with the cameraman that you are getting what you want. Then while the shot is being recorded the cameraman is on his own. You watch the monitor and if it's not what you want, you can suggest improvements and reshoot. The monitor gives you the chance of building up a close relationship with the cameraman very quickly – after the first few shots both of you are tuned in with each other's way of looking at things. It's a partnership which can take weeks to arrive at with film, where there is an unavoidable gap between shooting and viewing. In fact, many big-budget film productions now routinely offer the director a video monitor on location.

What should you look for on the monitor? Check where the main thing which you want to see is in the frame – is it too far away or lost in a jungle of other detail? (Television screens are small and so close-up shots on the whole look better than long shots.) Check round the edge of the frame: can you see anything you don't want to see, like a camera box or half of an interested bystander who shouldn't be in the shot? Check the lighting. Check that cables are tucked away out of shot. Check that people don't have plants growing out of the tops of their heads or lines through their ears (the camera flattens scenes).

Remember that the world you see on the screen differs from the world you see with your eyes. The difference is worth studying carefully. The central section of the zoom lens with which the camera is most comfortable (distortions creep in at both ends of the zoom) offers a much more narrow angle view of the world than your eyes. The camera is squeezing a three-dimensional world into a two-dimensional picture and so its view of the world is flatter than yours; you have to compensate by using lighting and sound, objects in the foreground and receding features in the background (like a road stretching into the distance) to give depth to your shots. The camera also gives equal emphasis to everything in the picture, unlike your eyes, which are directed by the brain to concentrate on specific parts of your field of vision.

So your task as a director is to choose what you want the viewers to look at. Then set up shots in which you (like the brain) direct the viewers' eyes to concentrate on specific parts by lighting, sound, camera angle and movement, the position of things in the picture and so on*.

*More about this in Briefing No. 13

It sounds a bit frightening at first but if you bear in mind that there is a difference between your view and the camera's view of the world and get into the habit of viewing things as the camera views them, you should avoid the most obvious

Use the monitor to check that the cameraman's idea of the shot is the same as your own

pitfalls. The video monitor is invaluable for this on locations where it's possible to have one – obviously a monitor would not be convenient if you were covering something like a protest-march. If you are using film, you can build up experience of the camera's view of the world by asking to look through the camera when the cameraman has lined up the shot.

using the tripod

One final point for this chapter: the tripod. For serious, professional programme-making the tripod is a necessity. It should be used for all shots unless there is a special reason for doing them hand-held (shooting a riot where speed is essential, doing a walking shot and so on). Some cameramen will insist that they can hold any shot rock-steady. Don't believe them: it's difficult with long shots; more difficult with mid-shots; impossible with close-ups or if you're panning or zooming; and absolutely and completely impossible if you are shooting something which isn't moving, like a poster or a building.

Tactfully say to the cameraman, 'You may be able to hand-hold as steady as a rock, but please use the tripod anyway. I don't want to tire you out . . .'. It may slow down shooting a little if you use a tripod, but the time lost is insignificant, and the gain in picture quality enormous.

a tripod on wheels

If you are working in somewhere like a factory where there is a reasonably smooth floor, it's a good idea to use a tripod on wheels (also known as a 'rolling spider' or 'rolling spreader', or – my favourite – 'legs on wheels'). Your station probably has one; if not, suggest they buy one.

Don't accept Totter-style 'wobbly-vision' (in San Totta the cameramen don't even bother to take their tripods with them on location). Wobbly-vision is extremely unprofessional. It's also both unnecessary and avoidable.

56

Whole books can be written (and have been) on how to direct programmes. But you don't have to read them all to learn to direct; shooting experience and your own eyes are by far the best teachers. If you plan your shooting, work from the finished sequence on your mental TV, and learn from your mistakes, you will soon be on the right lines. There really is no better way to learn than by doing it.

But there's no getting away from it – videorecording and filming are hard work. You have to keep thinking all the time, and a lapse of concentration can cause problems later when editing. Don't worry – it's unlikely that you will get full satisfaction on **all** the points I have made, to begin with. You have to compromise with filming, as you have to with everything else. If you get 75 out of every 100 of your shooting decisions right, you're doing well.

SUMMARY

Location Shooting

The producer must go on location with the crew.

Tell the cameraman about the programme (even if he doesn't seem to want to know).

Shoot important scenes first.

Cover each action with a 'master' shot and then do close-ups and reaction shots.

Break down each action into shots by 'seeing' the cut sequence on your 'mental TV'.

Finish all the shots in one set-up before moving to the next.

Shoot appropriate alternatives to give your editor (and you) a chance to cut together something good. Shoot enough!

With video allow 'run-up' time to ensure trouble-free editing.

Don't forget
 – homework is important
 – every shot matters
 – GVs (general views)
 – to do an introductory shot for every interviewee
 – to avoid jump cuts
 – cutaways
 – wallpaper shots

- insert shots (slow down the action)
- to hold each end of the zoom for 'three-shots-for-the-price-of-one'
- you can't rely on the library to cover shots you miss
- overlaps for sound vision
- not to cross the line.

Sound

Keep the sound recordist informed for each shot.

Shoot sync sound.

Use a clapper board.

Eliminate off-camera sounds as far as possible.

If off-camera sounds are loud and persistent, move the location.

Lighting

Keep the number of lighting set-ups to the minimum.

Tell the cameraman what sort of lighting you want.

Make sure lighting draws attention to the main object in the picture.

Avoid double shadows on noses.

Get rid of dark shadows on the back wall by moving the interviewee forward.

Check lighting by half closing your eyes.

Beware high contrast scenes

Special points for video

Don't shoot too much just because it's cheap.

Use a monitor on location whenever possible.

Check

- The right things in the picture stand out
- the edges of the picture
- lighting
- cables are out of sight
- composition.

Remember the camera doesn't see the world as you do.

Use a tripod (or tripod on wheels) whenever possible.

Banish 'wobbly-vision'.

Interviews

What is the worst interview you can imagine?

Virginia Donna managed to produce one for San TTV's 'Sixty Minute Profile' programme which would surely be the runaway winner if prizes were offered for awfulness.

*Guest and interviewee mean the same thing. To reduce the number of long words starting with 'inter . . .' I have used guest for studio interviews. It's clearer but unfortunately doesn't seem right for location interviews.

The guest*, a SanTA General (SanTA = San Totta Army), was very nervous. He read all his answers from a script (in shot throughout the interview), ploughed doggedly through each page while the viewers counted how many more pages there were to go. To hide his nervousness the General wore dark glasses and chain-smoked (lighting a new cigarette was a problem as he had nowhere to put down his script). Virginia, who likes to do the important interviews herself, ploughed through her long written list of questions as methodically as if the General were applying for a driving licence, and never thought of following up any interesting points the General made by asking a question not on the list. Indeed the opening questions sounded as if they had in fact been taken from an application form: what is your name? where do you work? how many people work in your office?

You must admit it takes talent to set up an interview as disastrous as this. But not all the credit should go to Virginia – part at least must be given to the General. It takes two to make – or muck up – an interview.

Let's look at some of the problems.

Scripted Interviews
Scripted interviews seem to flourish only in countries where broadcasting is in its infancy. Management, producers and the public all approach the medium with special reverence (like the radio announcers who wore dinner jackets in the early days of the BBC in Britain). The assumption seems to be that the medium is so important that it would be wrong just to answer questions in a normal way; every reply has to be rehearsed as carefully as a welcoming speech for a VIP. The result is boredom for the viewer. From where he is sitting the scripted interview is a sort of television growing pain: he has to take the pain while television does the growing.

How can you convince your guest that reading answers from a script really is a pain for viewers? There are several arguments you can use.

59

TV is intimate

Try reminding him that the point of the interview is to allow viewers to see him as a natural person expressing himself in a natural way, using language that they can understand. Television is an intimate medium. If you want to address the viewers effectively you have to speak as if you were addressing each person individually, and not pretend you are making a speech to an audience of thousands. If you script your answers in advance, you lose this intimacy and distance yourself from the viewer.

drawbacks of written language

Reading scripts so that they come to life and sound natural is also not easy; for it to be done successfully you need an actor, not an interviewee. Furthermore, when people write things down – as opposed to just talk about them naturally – they inevitably start using more formal, complicated language. The result is that a surprisingly high proportion of the less well-educated viewers simply won't understand what is being said (this is a problem which many television stations pretend doesn't exist).

These arguments may work. If they don't, try another line of attack: look at the problem from the guest's point of view. Ask him why he wants to use his script.

There are probably two reasons.

Firstly, he's frightened of forgetting what to say, of drying up. You can always assure him that you will remind him of what he's talking about, should his mind go blank at a crucial moment.

Persuade the guest not to use a script

The second reason the guest will probably give for wanting to hang on to his script is that he's frightened of saying the wrong thing. If the interview is a recorded one, you can easily deal with this fear by offering to do the interview again – or to edit it – if the guest is not happy.

If the interview is going to be transmitted live, and the guest refuses to be parted from his script, you have three more possible lines of attack.

Firstly, refuse to do the interview. This sort of shock tactic quite often works. But of course if like Virginia Donna you are dealing with a powerful VIP like the General (and don't relish the idea of facing a firing squad), then this isn't a realistic option.

So try another argument. Suggest your guest makes notes on a card of the important points he wants to get across and does the interview with only those notes before him.

If this doesn't work, try suggesting that since scripted interviews are so ineffective with the television audience, he might like to put his message across in the form of a statement to camera. This may well be the neatest solution of all since it forces both producer and guest to decide exactly what needs to be said and how to say it. And it's also over more quickly. But remember the point about using formal written language (which people may not understand) and keep to the simple words.

Of course the statement to camera solution wouldn't have worked for Virginia Donna and her 'Sixty Minute Profile' of the General; the sort of things Virginia wanted from the interview (opinions, reminiscences and anecdotes) are not the sort of things which come across well in a 'formal' statement.

Poor Virginia. The General's insistence on using a script turned the programme into a disaster, something which both the nervous General and Virginia could have done without (as Virginia should not have hesitated to point out). But you can't play tennis with a man who refuses to hold a racquet . . . . Don't ever allow yourself to be caught in this type of situation.

Dark Glasses
You know how irritating it is to have anything beyond the briefest of conversations with someone wearing dark glasses. On television dark glasses are even more irritating. The viewer is already deprived of most of the information he normally picks up from a person's body and hands because the 'talking head' is the most common shot on television. Now the dark glasses deprive him of the information from the eyes as well. And it's the eyes which are by far the most interesting part of the face: if the eyes aren't visible, the face seems to conceal more than it communicates. So you should use all your powers of persuasion to get the interviewee to take off his dark glasses.

Remember also, when interviewing outside, that bright sunlight can cast deep shadows under the eyebrows which will hide the eyes as effectively as dark glasses; on the screen there will be just two black holes where the eyes ought to be. You can reproduce the effect by looking through half-shut eyes at a face lit by a midday sun high in the sky.

To avoid this, put your interviewee in front of a darker background or – if the sun is directly overhead – you may have to record with the interviewee looking slightly upwards (have the interviewer standing and the interviewee sitting).

Smoking

cigarettes

Warning: cigarettes can seriously damage your interview as well as your interviewee. And the damage to your programme – like the damage to health – only shows up later.

At the time of recording the interview, smoking may seem a good idea. It relaxes the interviewee, gives him something to do with his hands, and makes him look natural. The snags only show up when you try and shorten the interview by dropping a section. Invariably you find then that the two shots won't cut because in one shot your interviewee has a cigarette in his mouth and in the next shot he hasn't. Or vice versa.

You also discover then that a burning cigarette in shot acts like a clock for the viewer: it gives him a way of measuring the passage of time in your picture. So as the cigarette grows shorter (or even longer) with each edit the viewer starts thinking more about what you've left out than what you've left in . . .

pipes

Pipe-smoking is safer for your programme, as well as for your health. At least the viewer can't guess the passing of time from a pipe. Though you can bet that if you want to edit the interview the pipe will be in different places in the two shots you want to join together.

cigars

Cigars are in a sort of half-way house – less trouble than cigarettes (they burn more slowly) and more trouble than pipes (they are in and out of the mouth more often).

Of course all these problems only arise if you want to edit the interview later.

Questions

Let's assume that like Virginia you have decided to ask the questions yourself in an interview. On the whole it is better to have someone else to do this for you, particularly if you are still fairly new as a producer; you will find that you have more than enough to do just organising and directing the interview without trying to ask the questions as well. But you should know how to prepare and use questions for an interview, and so let's assume you are doing it all yourself.

The first point to consider is whether you should be doing an interview at all. Is the story or information you hope to get from your interviewee best suited to be brought out in an interview? Would it work better in commentary, or put over as a piece to camera?

If your interviewee has done something himself or has an eyewitness account of something, or you are asking for his opinion, fine. But if for example he is merely giving you a summary of a report or something second-hand, wouldn't it perhaps be more effective to put the information into the commentary? Or get a good journalist to write a short witty summary in simple language and deliver it straight to camera instead of doing an interview? Journalists are usually good at doing this; most members of the public aren't.

make a list

But you have decided that an interview would be appropriate. Write out in note form a list of the questions which you would like to ask. If you are doing, for example, a short interview about a new tyre-making machine, your list might go something like this:

– why is the new machine needed?

– reaction of the workers in the factory

– what benefit for motorists?

You need write out in full only your first question. Keep the rest in note form. You will find as the interview progresses that your mind automatically rephrases each of the following questions to take into account what the interviewee has already said, so that your questions sound natural and spontaneous. Having the questions in note form also stops you rehearsing the next question to yourself when you should be listening to the interviewee's answers. This in turn avoids another bad mistake (which can happen all too easily if you aren't listening) – the mistake of asking a question which the interviewee has already answered. It's this sort of mistake which makes the interviewee wonder if you know what you are doing.

supplementaries

It's well worth following up interesting points in the interviewee's answers (even if they take you into areas which you haven't foreseen on your list) by asking extra or supplementary questions. But beware of straying far from the planned course of the interview.

foresee likely answers

It's a good idea also to think ahead while preparing for the interview about what sort of answers you are going to get to your questions. My first question about the tyre-making machine ('Why is it needed?') is designed to get the interviewee talking. He can't really answer the question without first telling the viewer something about the machine it is replacing, what the drawbacks of that machine were, the advantages of the new machine and so on. In short, he has to explain a lot about the background to the change before he can answer the actual question in a way which makes sense to anyone who isn't an expert in tyre production. (If he doesn't do the explaining required, you should be asking him a series of short supplementaries to make sure he does.)

So the question 'Why is the new machine needed?' is likely to produce an informative answer. Questions like 'Will the machine be good for your business?' and 'How much does the machine cost?' are not likely to produce answers of any interest. It would be a stupid businessman indeed who introduced a machine which he thought would be **bad** for his business. Similarly, the actual price of the machine is just a figure which means nothing unless it is unexpectedly high or low. 'About as much as you would expect' would be an accurate – if rather rude – answer.

A better question about the cost might be: 'This machine has cost you one million dollars. With tyres dropping in price and lasting longer than ever, are you likely ever to get your money back?' Questions like 'How much does the machine cost?' are 'How long is a piece of string?' questions. The answer by itself is of no interest unless it is unexpected or makes a comparison. So avoid this sort of question by thinking about likely answers at the same time as you are thinking about questions.

'How do you feel about . . .?' questions

Another type of commonly used question which it is better to avoid is the 'How do you feel about . . .?' question. 'How did you feel when you saw your granny falling over the cliff?' The question is itself so unfeeling that you almost wish the interviewee would reply 'How do you think I felt?'

More usually the 'How do you feel about . . .?' question stimulates the interviewee into saying nothing more interesting than a few adjectives. 'How do you feel about having your savings stolen?' – 'Er . . . poorer.' Notice that if the interviewee does start to say something more interesting, it's because he's chosen to ignore the question and answer one you haven't put.

It's far better to ask questions which help the interviewee through his story. For example, 'Did your granny know there was a cliff there?' and 'Were the savings which were stolen from under the bed the only ones you had?'

It is very easy to slip into using the 'How-do-you-feel-about?' question because it's such an all-purpose fishing net for people's opinions and feelings. But when you find it springing to mind, stop and think. A more closely defined question will get a better answer.

Questions to avoid

Other questions which you should avoid are questions which are too general ('Has your grandmother's death changed your views on the meaning of life?'); double questions ('How did the thief get into your house and do you think the police will catch him?'); questions which go on so long that they sound more like answers; and questions which are really answers in disguise and leave the guest with nothing worthwhile to say ('This accident to your grandmother – obviously a terrible shock and surprise – must have left you drained of emotion. How else has it affected you?').

Finally, with a location interview you often want to get answers which you can use without keeping the questions in the finished programme. This means that your interviewee must not answer 'yes' or 'no' and should ideally repeat the subject of the question in his answer. This can be difficult to explain to the interviewee, and can make him quite nervous, since it feels stilted and unnatural to answer a question like 'Is the machine working as well as you hoped?' by saying 'The new machine is working well' instead of the far more natural 'Yes, it's fine . . . .'

getting self-contained answers

There are two ways of getting a self-contained answer which doesn't start with 'yes' or 'no'. The first is to start your question with either Who, What, When, Where, Which, Why, or How; none of these invites a 'yes' or 'no' answer.

The other way is not to ask a question at all. Instead use the formula 'Tell me . . .' For example, 'Tell me how well the new machine is working.' The answer is almost bound to be self-contained without a 'yes' or 'no'. And if your interviewee answers 'It's working well' instead of repeating the subject – 'The new machine is working well' – it will almost certainly be clear from the context in the finished programme what he is talking about. Anyway you can always mention the new machine in your commentary leading up to his answer.

Two other useful variations of the 'Tell me . . .' formula are

1   to state the subject in advance. For example, 'The new machine, tell me how it's working.'
2   use the formula 'Let's talk about . . .' For example, 'Let's talk about your new machine and how well it's working.'

You can no doubt invent for yourself other ways of getting answers in self-contained statements.

Before You Start
Your interviewee has agreed to throw away his script, take off his dark glasses and stop smoking. You should do the

same – except for one thing. Don't let go of your list of questions.

keep your list of questions

It might seem inconsistent that you should keep these when the interviewer has had to drop his script completely. But your situations are really quite different. The interviewee should be familiar enough with what he is talking about to answer questions without notes; it's far more difficult for you to remember the list of all the points you want to raise. After all, the list of possible questions is very long; the list of truthful answers to each question is very short.

the run-through with the interviewee

You should run through the list of areas you want to talk about and discuss each briefly with the interviewee before you start recording. Let him think for a moment about the answers he would like to give. In some cases he might even suggest a different point to raise and there is no reason why you shouldn't accept this if it seems sensible. This run-through is **not** a rehearsal. It's just a quick recce of the field of discussion so that the interviewee knows which way he's going; he's likely to perform much more effectively and confidently if he's got his bearings than if he's blundering about lost and under fire from you. Unless of course you are doing an interview which is trying to expose the interviewee's weaknesses . . . .

Let me emphasise that this run-through mustn't turn into a word-by-word rehearsal of the whole interview. If it does, you'll find that when you and the interviewee repeat it for the camera your second efforts will probably have lost the freshness of the first.

nervous interviewees

The one exception to this rule is a trick you can play on interviewees who are particularly nervous. If the cameraman and sound recordist are ready, quietly tell them to start recording. Then tell the interviewee that you'll do a complete rehearsal with him so that he has nothing to worry about when he does the 'proper' interview. This 'rehearsal' is probably the best interview you'll get out of him. If you think you can do better there's nothing to stop you shooting the 'proper' interview as well. Even with an interviewee who's not particularly nervous there's nothing to stop you going over parts of the interview again if you think that he can improve on his first answers.

Finish your run-through with the interviewee by telling him to keep his answers fairly brief and to the point. If he is a man of few words and is likely to give you one-word answers only, remind him that your questions are intended to prompt him to talk; you don't want to have to drag out every fact and opinion by cross-examining him like a witness in a courtroom. Finally, remind him to talk to you and not to the camera. In fact he shouldn't worry about the camera at all.

A last check now of one or two technical points. Is there a nasty black shadow on the wall behind the interviewee? If there is, discuss with the cameraman how best to remove it. The sound man will want to have a little bit of talk from both you and the interviewee to check the voice levels (if he hasn't done so already). The traditional way of getting the interviewee to talk for a voice test is to ask him what he had for breakfast. A question about some other subject (not the subject of the interview) may relax the interviewee more and give you a better idea of how your interviewee will talk and behave on camera. Then take any nearby telephones that are not in the shot off the hook so that they don't ring in the middle of your interview. Put the clapperboard on the beginning of the shot, allow the cameraman time to refocus on the interviewee and you're off with your first question . . ..

Interview Shooting Techniques
The thing to avoid in interviews is the profile. Profile shots (those where only one eye of the interviewee is visible) look and feel awkward. The viewer soon feels deprived, as if he had bought the cheapest seat in the theatre and has only a restricted view of the stage. You should put your viewers in the best seats in the house. So the thing to aim for is shots of both the interviewer and guest which show both their eyes.

There are two distinct techniques for getting these shots. Which one you use depends on how many cameras you have available.

1   *The One-Camera Technique*
It is impossible to get two people talking to each other in one shot without one of them being in profile. The only way it could work would be if both of them talked without looking at each other. But people can't do that for more than a few minutes without strain (try it with a friend). In normal situations people face each other when they talk.

It follows therefore that if you have only one camera, you can successfully film only one person at a time. So you should of course start with the interviewee. Place him in front of the camera. Then – and this is the crucial point – place the interviewer **next** to the camera. The interviewee will naturally look at him while he's talking and the camera will have a nice comfortable shot of the interviewee's face with two eyes showing.

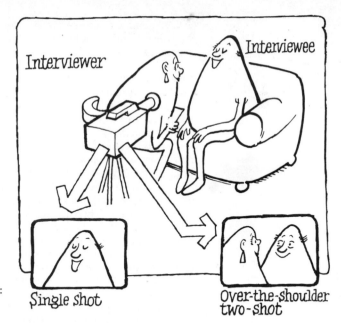

Single shot

Over-the-shoulder two-shot

One-Camera Technique: Interviewer next to the camera

over-the-shoulder two-shot

If the interviewer takes a step forward from his position next to the camera and the cameraman widens his shot a little, you have a useful two-shot showing the interviewee's face (as before) and the back of the interviewer's head and shoulder on one side of the picture. This shot is known as the 'over-the-shoulder two-shot' and is often used as an opening shot for an interview (the camera zooms in to a mid-shot of the interviewee as he starts his first answer).

2   *The Two-camera or Studio Technique*
    If you have more than one camera for an interview (as you do in the studio) the positioning of your interviewer and guest is quite different. This time they both sit in front of the cameras, slightly apart with chairs at right-angles for most interviews, and directly opposite each other for argumentative confrontation interviews. The cameras then 'cross-shoot' – that is, each camera takes a shot of the person who is furthest away so that the fields of vision of the two cameras appear to cross (hence the name 'cross-shoot'). If they don't cross-shoot they will be getting profile shots.

    Both cameras can also get an over-the-shoulder two-shot if they move round slightly but cutting between two-shots from each camera can be unpleasant – the jump isn't smooth, even if both shots are well matched. So use only one two-shot at a time.

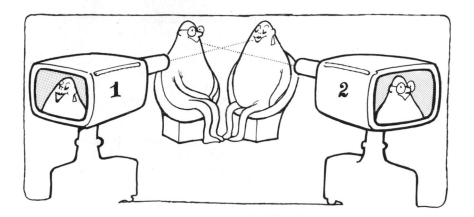

Two-Camera or Studio Technique: Cross-shoot

the third camera

If you have a third camera (not really necessary) you can position it half-way between the other two cameras and a little behind them, so that it gives you a long two-shot with interviewer and guest evenly balanced on either side of the picture. This is the shot you should set up first in your studio rehearsal time, as it determines the position of the chairs more than the shots from the other two cameras. It's probable that when you try this shot you will find your two people are sitting too far apart and you will have to move their chairs closer together to get both of them into one shot. They may in fact have to sit closer together than feels natural, in some cases with their knees almost touching. But unnatural though this may feel to them, it usually looks all right to the viewer. For this two-shot the participants will be in profile, but this is acceptable for a short time in long shot.

You can also put your third camera next to your first or second one to give you a two-shot favouring either guest or interviewer. Opinions differ about whom it's best to favour. Normally one would say it's best to favour the guest but the cut from two-shot favouring the guest to single-shot of the guest isn't very attractive. On the other hand the two-shot favouring the interviewer is useful for questions and cuts well with the single-shot of the guest answering.

Special Points for Studio Interviews
Studio interviews differ from film interviews in more than just shooting techniques. There are other points to be noted.

1   MAKE-UP   Both interviewer and guest should have their faces lightly made up. At the very least they should have a dusting of face powder to stop any perspiration glistening under the studio lights.

2   NERVES   Being interviewed in the studio is far more frightening than being interviewed on location. The guest finds himself on strange territory away from familiar surroundings. The studio lights glare down at him from the ceiling; he's surrounded by cameras which look none too friendly. He is also the only person who can't hear what's being said on the talk-back. It all makes him feel like the chief victim at a sacrifice.

So he needs especially friendly attention. If you are the only person in the production team whom he's met before, make a point of going on to the studio floor and showing him to his seat. Remind him of the interviewer's name (in case he's forgotten) and introduce him to the floor manager. Tell him that the interviewer and floor manager will look after him when you have returned to the gallery and remember to ask the floor manager to keep him informed about what's happening when the inevitable delays occur.

I have already mentioned the trick of recording the 'rehearsal' if your guest is very nervous. Sometimes nerves may take the form of an inability to stop talking, in which case the interviewer must firmly and politely interrupt the guest to get him back to answering the question.

It is important that the interviewer always keeps his temper under control and behaves politely, even if he has a guest who isn't controlled and well-behaved. The one thing which the interviewer must avoid at all costs is to appear to bully his guest. If he does so, the interviewer will quickly lose the sympathy of the viewers.

3   RESTARTING AN INTERVIEW   Many guests – even those who aren't particularly nervous – start off rather badly and then visibly improve as they relax, forget about the cameras and start concentrating on what they are saying. If you notice this happening and the interview is not going out live, stop the recording after the first two or three questions and answers and start again from the beginning. You will almost certainly find yourself with a much improved interview.

This idea is also worth trying for interviews on location.

4   SWIVEL CHAIRS   Some television problems are foreseeable and therefore avoidable; some are not. Swivel chairs belong to the first category. So refuse to have them in the studio. If you don't, you will one day be caught in a live broadcast with two artists who nervously jiggle backwards and forwards. The jiggling will attract more attention than the words and your viewers will remember little else.

5   JUMPING FLOWERPOTS   Think for a moment about the area between the interviewee and interviewer. It will appear in both their shots – on the left of one shot and on the right of the other. If you have something eyecatching in this area (like a vase of flowers), it will appear to jump from one side of the screen to the other with each cut. Avoid this unpleasant effect by moving the object to one side (so that it appears on only one of the shots), or by removing it completely from the set.

6   CLOSE-UPS OF OBJECTS   If the guest has brought something to the studio which you want to show in big close-up, you must decide during the rehearsal which camera should take the shot. Give it to the camera which is normally on the interviewer (if you have only two cameras); the camera on the guest is the most important camera you have got and it is always dangerous to take it off him.

You must rehearse this close-up before you start the interview, as the cameraman won't be able to get a good shot unless he knows exactly what is going to happen. So ask your guest to hold the object in the way he expects to do when talking about it. Then try and get a close-up on your chosen camera. You will almost certainly have to ask the guest to move the object slightly before you are satisfied. Once you are, make it clear to him (through the floor manager) that it's very important that he holds it in exactly the same position during the interview. Remind him also (if you feel it's not too much to ask of him as an amateur) to make all his hand movements slow and clear. Then pray that he remembers these points – guests often forget.

If you want a very big close-up you may find that the guest cannot hold the object still enough and you will have to put the object on a table or even move it to a stand in another part of the studio. On location, of course, the problem is not so difficult. You do the close-up after the interview and as you don't need any sound you can direct the interviewee to position and move the object as you wish while you are shooting. The close-up can then be inserted as required during editing.

7   CUTTING AND SHOT SIZES   In studio interviews it is very tempting to change shot more often than necessary simply because you have two or more cameras. Resist this temptation. Use the optional shots at your disposal only if the interview will be improved by them, not just because they are there. Your cuts should be motivated by the subtle changes of mood which take place as the interview progresses.

This means that you don't have to cut back to the interviewer for every question. You also don't have to cut to a long two-shot in the middle of an interesting answer just to show that you can. This doesn't mean you should do the whole interview on one shot. By all means make full use of the shots you have available, but make sure that they serve the content of the interview (technique is the servant, not the master).

match shot size with mood

The way to do this is to listen to what your artists are saying. If the conversation is becoming interesting, move in to close-up; if it's amusing, show a quick reaction shot of the interviewer being amused. Mid-shots for relaxed answers, medium close-ups and close-ups (the most useful shots) for more important answers, big close-ups if the subject is confessing something or under pressure. The more fascinating you find the answer, the closer-up the shot should be. And the closer-up the shot, the fuller face it should be. Close-up profiles are contradictory; you are cutting closer to show the viewers more, yet the profile shows them less. The only exception is if you have a verbal battle in the studio. Then two close-up profiles in quick succession could be effective.

You can develop the sensitivity to match shots with moods by observing people talking in normal life where the way they look (or don't look) at each other is always changing to suit the mood. Lovers tend to exchange sweet nothings in close-up. It would appear very odd if you bought a bus ticket in the same way. Unless of course you were being hunted by the police and were desperately scanning the bus conductor's face to see if he recognised you.

avoid zooming out

The shot of the interviewer should be roughly the same size as that of the guest at any one time. Zooming in to a person talking is perfectly acceptable. But zooming out while a person talks is not: it looks like you are walking out on him in mid-sentence. If you want to go to a wider shot, cut to your interviewer for a reaction shot or question and then cut back to a wider shot of your guest.

8   HOW TO AVOID LATE CUTS   It's easy when you are cutting between interviewer and guest to miss the first few words of a question and the first few words of an answer. The trick here is to watch the monitor of the person who isn't speaking while listening to the person who is. People normally wind themselves up before they speak. If you look out for the tell-tale signs (the back stiffens slightly, the jaw drops a fraction) while listening for the pause in the speaker's flow (which the interviewer in the studio is also waiting for) you

will find it a lot easier to time your cuts correctly. It seems odd at first watching the person who isn't speaking and it requires a deliberate effort but with practice it soon becomes a habit. Of course, there is no reason why the vision mixer shouldn't take the cuts for you during an interview, with you setting the course of the proceedings: for example, 'stay with the guest for the next question' or 'take the next question on (camera) two'.

9 RECORDING INSERT INTERVIEWS If you are recording an interview in the studio for later use as an insert in a magazine programme, it's a good idea to start and end the interview with a shot of the guest and not the interviewer. This is specially helpful if the interviewer is also presenting the magazine programme since it avoids potential horrors such as the presenter (live) introducing himself (recorded) in the next shot. The same unpleasantness can occur if you end your interview with a shot of the interviewer and he then has to introduce the next item live from the studio.

10 STUDIO CUTAWAYS If you expect to edit a recorded interview, it's worth doing listening shots of both interviewer and guest **before** the main interview. These can be done unobtrusively while the interviewer is talking to the guest to put him at his ease, and while the guest is answering a couple of questions (about something other than the topic for the interview) to give the sound supervisor a chance to balance voice levels. Listening shots done after the interview always seem to be a bit of a chore for the participants. So it's worth getting them out of the way first.

More about studios in Chapter 11 and Briefing No. 1

Special Points for One-camera Interviews

1 SHOT SIZES When you are using the one-camera technique you should discuss with the cameraman the shot sizes you want before starting the interview. Tell him the questions which you expect to produce answers most suitable for close-ups but it is best to let him use his own judgement about when to move in close during the interview. It's best also to ask him to change shot sizes during the questions so that you can edit the answers without worrying about camera movements.

2 CUTAWAYS If you want to edit interviews shot with the one-camera technique you will need cutaways. There are two types of these: listening shots (sometimes known as 'noddies') and cutaway questions.

interviewee's listening shots

The easiest cutaway to do is the over-the-shoulder two-shot described on page 68 which you can use as a cutaway over a question. All you have to do is ask the interviewer to talk to the interviewee (about anything which doesn't make him laugh). The interviewee just has to listen. Don't bother to ask him to nod as he will probably overdo it.

interviewer's listening shots

In fact, when you take cutaway shots of the interviewer it's also a good idea to tell him not to nod too much. Too many nods quickly begin to look silly. All that is required is that the interviewer should not stand or sit there looking as motionless as a waxwork; a slight movement of the head or eyes or a shifting of weight from one side to the other is all that is needed for a usable listening cutaway.

shooting the interviewer's cutaways

The obvious way to shoot a listening cutaway of the interviewer is to put the camera in the opposite position you had it for the interview – in other words, position it so that this time the interviewee is slightly to the front and next to the camera. From this position you can shoot the interviewer listening and then you can also zoom out for an over-the-shoulder two-shot. For the two-shot it is best to get the interviewee talking (even though you can't see his face) so that the interviewer has something to listen to.

cutaway questions

With the camera in this position (next to the interviewee) you can take shots of the interviewer repeating the most important questions, in single or in two-shot as you wish. Discuss with your interviewer which questions are best. You don't need to repeat all of them and should try and choose ones at points where you think you will want to edit. Then keep the recorder rolling while he goes through them one by one (with you prompting him if necessary). If the questions during the interview were a bit loose and rambling this is a good opportunity to make them shorter and more effective.

For a short interview you don't of course have to do all four possible cutaways each time. Often the two-shot with the interviewee listening while the interviewer talks, some listening shots from the interviewer and a few cutaway questions will be more than enough. If you can remember to record all your cutaways on a different videotape (not the interview tape) you will save yourself a lot of spooling forwards and back during editing.

a quicker way to do interviewer's cutaways

If you want only single-shot cutaways of your interviewer you needn't go to all the trouble of moving camera and lights to face exactly the opposite direction. Instead just pan the camera slightly so that it shows a different background – who is to know if it wasn't the interviewer's actual background during the interview? Make sure that the interviewer is looking towards the right of camera if the interviewee was looking left (or vice versa).

the long shot as cutaway

You can also use a long shot of the interview as a cutaway provided it is far enough away to prevent the viewer seeing if the shot is in sync or not. This is usually possible only when you are doing an interview outdoors. Sometimes for very relaxed interviews a change of camera position can also give you opportunities to edit without breaking the flow of the talk with a cutaway.

eyelines

Generally speaking, for interviews the camera lens should be level with the eyes of the person in the shot. If interviewer and guest are roughly the same size and are sitting at the same height, this is straightforward. If size or heights differ, the camera should try and reflect this by adopting the point of view of each participant and looking up or down on the person in shot as appropriate. But beware. Looking down on people makes them look inferior (that's what the word means); looking up makes them look superior. You may want to introduce these slants for dramatic effect but before you do, ask yourself if they will help or hinder what is said in the interview. Remember also that looking up at ladies rarely flatters them; it tends to make their jawbone look unattractively large and they won't thank you for drawing attention to their double chins if they have any! Ladies should also be advised not to wear off-the-shoulder evening dresses without straps when appearing on television, as close-ups will give the impression that they have no clothes on at all.

Looking up at ladies
rarely flatters them

SUMMARY

Interviews

Scripted Interviews   Avoid at all costs – they aren't natural and many viewers won't understand the formal written language.

With *recorded* interviews reassure the interviewee that you can repeat the interview (or parts of it) if he forgets what to say or says the wrong thing

With *live* interviews try

– refusing to do the interview (risky, but often works)

– suggesting the interviewee uses notes instead of a script

– suggesting (if all else fails) a short statement to camera (at least it's over quicker)

Dark Glasses and Smoking   Avoid.

Questions　　First ask yourself if you should be doing an interview at all. Would commentary or a statement to camera be more effective?

Write out the first question and note areas for further discussion.

Don't be frightened of supplementaries.

Foresee likely answers.

Avoid:

– 'how long is a piece of string?' questions

– 'how do you feel about . . .?' questions

– questions which are too general

– double questions

– overlong questions

– questions which are answers in disguise.

For self-contained answers (which don't start with 'yes' or 'no') start questions with either Who, What, When, Where, Which, Why or How.

Or use the formulas 'Tell me . . .' or 'Let's talk about. . .'

Before you Start　　Run through with the interviewee what you intend to ask him. But don't rehearse the interview word by word.

With nervous interviewees perhaps record a full-scale 'rehearsal'.

Ask long-winded interviewees to be brief; ask men of few words to give full answers. Remind both to talk to the interviewer, not to the camera.

Check the shadow on the back wall.

Let the sound recordist check voice levels.

Take nearby telephones off the hook.

Put on the clapper-board. You're off!

Interview Shooting Techniques

One-camera Technique – interviewer next to the camera.

Two-camera Technique – cross-shoot.

Special Points for Studio Interviews

Don't forget make-up.

Interviewees find television studios strange and frightening. Reassure them

Interviewer must always be firm, polite and never bully – even when provoked.

If the interview starts badly, start again after the interviewee has settled down by answering two or three questions.

Swivel chairs and jumping flowerpots: avoid.

Close-ups of objects: use the interviewer's – or the third – camera.

Motivate all your cuts. Match shot sizes with mood.

Avoid zooming out from people while they are talking.

To avoid cutting late watch the monitor of the person who isn't talking.

Start and end insert interviews with a shot of the guest.

Record listening cutaways before the interview if possible.

Special Points for One-camera Interviews

Shot Sizes. Let cameraman use his own judgement during the interview but warn him before where close-up material is likely to occur. Ask him to change shot sizes over questions.

Cutaways. Two types: listening shots ('noddies') and cutaway questions.

– do over-the shoulder two-shot for interviewee's listening shot

– put camera behind interviewee for interviewer's cutaways

– or just pan camera to show different background for interviewer. Record some cutaway questions (better expressed than the originals if possible) and listening shots.

– record cutaways on a different videotape to save editing time.

You can also use long shots or changes of camera angle to edit interviews.

Don't shoot from above or below eyeline height without good reason.

Avoid shooting ladies from low angles.

Off-the-shoulder evening dresses without straps can give an unfortunate impression in closer shots.

Editing

The everyday word for editing is 'cutting'. But the best way of approaching this stage of the programme-making process is to think of it as 'selecting'. When you edit, you are selecting the best shots, and the best parts of the best shots for telling your story.

finding the natural lifespan of a shot

The key to editing is finding the precise point at which a shot starts being interesting and the precise point at which it stops being interesting. All shots have a natural lifespan. You should learn to identify this by looking at each shot and asking yourself, 'Which bit works best?' With static shots in which nothing much is moving – for example, a shot of an oil tanker on the horizon – the cut-off point comes quite quickly. You can lengthen the lifespan of this shot a little by drawing attention to some aspect of it in the commentary – for example, by saying something about oil slicks on the water. But if you want to continue to talk about oil slicks you will need a close-up of them; your first shot has reached the end of its natural lifespan and it will become boring if you prolong it.

With moving shots the natural lifespan may be considerably longer. For example, you have a car filling the shot and the viewer sees that the car is big, expensive and very clean. He notices a flag fluttering from the bonnet and then sees the shadowy outline of what looks like a VIP sitting behind the driver. The shot begins to widen and he notices the scenery which the car is driving through. The camera continues to pull out and he sees that the car is stopping at a petrol station. Obviously this shot will hold the interest of the viewer for a lot longer than the static shot of the tanker, because at each stage of its development it offers the viewer something new to look at.

The lifespan of a shot is also affected by the neighbouring shots. Clearly, a close-up of the tanker on the horizon following the long shot would affect how long you keep the long shot on the screen.

Editing, of course, is not just finding the natural lengths of individual shots; you also have to find a way of putting them all together to tell the story. The procedures for doing this are rather different for film and video and so I will deal with them separately. It is logical to start with film because that is the older craft from which modern practices with video are derived.

Editing Film

First check that your film editor has received all the film you have shot and all the sound you have recorded; Totta films are frequently 'cut' by a third or more before they get anywhere near the cutting room because the rolls aren't clearly labelled and are therefore lost.

synchronise picture and sound

Then make sure that the editor or his assistant synchronises as much of the sound with the picture as possible. Of course this isn't necessary if the film has been shot on commag (or stripe) film where the sound is recorded on a thin magnetic stripe next to the picture and is in sync anyway. The only snag with editing commag, however, is that the picture runs 28 frames behind the sound; a cut at the point in the picture where a presenter is starting a piece to camera will remove just over a second's worth of his words (about three words), and a cut at the point where the sound begins will show just over a second's worth of him standing there about to begin. The way round this problem is to transfer all commag sound on to a separate magnetic track for editing. This sepmag sound (as it is usually called) can then be synchronised with the picture in the normal way before you start editing the film. Or if you have to edit on commag, shoot the statement to camera with the presenter starting to talk while out of shot and then zoom out or pan to reveal him (or have him walk into shot).

How do you keep picture and sound in sync while cutting? The answer is always to add or drop exactly the same number of frames from both rolls, adding spacing where necessary – for example where there's no sound for a picture.

key and rubber numbers

There are also two other systems for keeping sync: key numbers and rubber numbers. Key (or edge) numbers are built into the edge of the film stock by the manufacturer and are automatically printed through on to any copies; if you are using negative, key numbers are indispensable for matching up the cutting copy with the master negative. Rubber numbers are printed on to both picture and sepmag after they have been synchronised; they provide an accurate, easy way of getting picture and sound back in sync if for any reason they have come adrift. Of course, both systems can also be used to reunite short pieces of picture or sound with their original neighbours provided the short piece has a number on it. If it's less than about 20 frames long (the standard interval for printing numbers) you could be out of luck.

Occasionally you may have an editor who says that it will save time to edit the picture first and then put in the sync sound later. Try and discourage him. Finding the right bits of sync sound to go with edited shots is a lengthy task which can take up more time than you saved by not doing it in the first place (when it is in fact much easier). Anyway the sound is often an important element in determining the lifespan of a shot. Think of a racing car revving up before a race: how is the editor going to do justice to this shot if he doesn't consider picture and sound together?

Once everything has been synchronised sit down with the editor and view everything you have shot, explaining to the editor what it is about and how you want to use it. Also make a list of the roll, shot and take number of each shot and a short description of what's in it, if you don't already have one. This shot list can save you a lot of time and temper later when you are desperately looking for particular shots. Then go away and write down the order in which you want the shots assembled. 'Ah,' you may ask, 'why not use the order in the treatment?' The reason is that it's extremely rare that your shots have turned out as you expected.

Shots which you slaved over while filming can turn out to be lifeless and rather ordinary; shots you did as second best can turn out to be marvellous. So it's important to look at all the shots with as unbiased an eye as possible, forgetting all the behind-the-scenes stories of what went into getting them. Your film editor can be a great help in this. He is in fact your first viewer and he can also offer you the enormous advantage of seeing your shots with both the eye of experience and the eye of one who comes fresh to your story. So listen to what he has to say – if he's a good editor he's worth his weight in gold as a judge of your material.

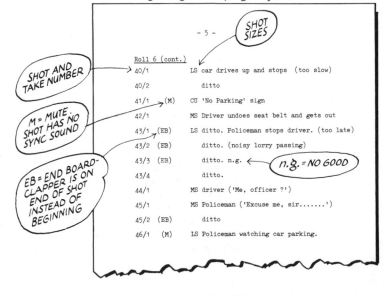

Shot list

picture problems

Your first viewing with the film editor is also the time when
you learn about camera and cameraman problems which you
hadn't realised existed. If you are unlucky, some of your
shots may be unsteady or badly composed or not held long
enough or have dirt on the picture. These disasters may
come as a shock to you, but don't retaliate by making a
savage complaint about the cameraman (certainly not if you
are still a new producer). Remember that the cameraman's
mistakes all show up in the picture; your mistakes aren't
nearly as eye-catching. If you couldn't make up your mind
about a shot on location, the cameraman probably made up
your mind for you. If he couldn't make up his mind on
location, there is almost certainly a fault in the shot to show
for it.

**view shots as early as
possible**

It's a good idea to check your shots for any problems even
before you have finished all your days on location,
particularly if you're working with a cameraman who is new
to you. Arrange to have the previous day's footage shown to
you when you return to base after each day's filming and
invite the cameraman to view them also. Cameramen rarely
have the chance of seeing their shots before they are cut and
a quick spin through together (you can probably view most
of them at double speed without sound) will do wonders for
your understanding of each other. Of course if you are
working with video you have the advantage of being able to
review your shots instantly if you have any doubts.

81

the assembly order   But let's return to the film editor and the assembly order.
                            This can be very brief, just a list of shots with enough
                            information to identify them (roll, shot and take number
                            will be ample). By this time your editor should know what
                            you are after in the programme and so you don't need to
                            write too much down.

stay in the cutting   You should try and spend as much time with the editor as
room   possible because there is no better place than the cutting
                            room to learn about making films. The order in which you
                            assemble shots and sequences makes an enormous amount
                            of difference to the finished programme, and the only way to
                            learn to judge the impact of the various ways of joining up
                            film is by doing it. Your time in the cutting room will also
                            help you when you next go out filming, as you will then have
                            a much better idea of what shots are needed.

viewing the first   When the first assembly of the film is ready, sit down with
assembly   the editor and look through it non-stop without worrying
                            about details. This will give you an idea of the programme's
                            overall strength and weaknesses; discuss these with the
                            editor and think about ways of strengthening your weak
                            points and making more of your strong points. Is the overall
                            pace of the film too even (and therefore a little boring)? Are
                            your fast and lively sequences distributed to their best
                            advantage? Does each sequence contribute something
                            worthwhile to the story? Do you have a good sequence to
                            start with, and one almost as good to end with? Are there
                            some good patches in the middle?

pictures come first   Although you should think about the commentary while you
                            are cutting, don't let it dictate the order or length of the
                            shots. Films are not illustrated commentaries; the picture
                            must come first and the commentary second. There are only
                            two exceptions to this general rule:

1   when a news reporter records a commentary on location and
    sends it back with pictures which are then cut to fit the
    commentary;

2   when you decide to cut pictures to music (using it as a sort of
    commentary). For this you have to find the music first and
    then try and fit the pictures to the music.

    After considering the overall impact of the first assembly
    you should go over each sequence in detail with the editor,
    looking carefully at every shot and every cut and seeing if
    you can improve them. Here are some things to look out for:

check the length   1   Check that you have found the best possible length for each shot. Would it do its job as well if it were shorter? If so, trim it. Remember most films and shots suffer from being too long rather than too short.

are the cuts smooth?   2   Does each shot join up smoothly with its neighbours? The eye concentrates on only one point of the screen at a time – usually the brightest point, or the point where there is something moving (for example, the fly crawling up the newsreader's jacket). You can often make a cut smoother (and therefore better) by making sure that the points which attract the eye in neighbouring shots are in the same section of the screen.

Often jump cuts between locations (your reporter is inside the building in one shot, outside in the next) can be made to look acceptable by following this principle. But make sure the shot sizes are different, as cutting between the same size shots of a person or thing is always ugly. There's a particular danger of doing this in the studio where you have more cameras at your disposal.

If all else fails, a trick you could use to get round an awkward cut is to introduce a sudden, sharp noise on the sound track just before the offending cut – something like a car horn or a door slam. The viewers will blink involuntarily and miss the cut!

trim interviews   3   Trim the first question from the front of interviews; you can almost always set up what the interviewee is talking about in fewer words in the commentary. You will probably find also that your interviewee doesn't really start answering the question till about the third sentence in. If this is so, drop the first two sentences.

It's common too that the middle of the interviewee's answer contains the meat of what he wants to say and everything thereafter is a bit of trimming, or even a repeat of what he has just said. Do you need this extra bit? I am not suggesting you cut all interviews to shreds. But your programme will benefit enormously if you use only the meat of your interviews and trim the fat.

shots with camera   4   With camera movements trim off the static bits at each end
movement   and just use the moving part of the shot, unless there is a definite reason why you should keep both in. It looks odd for example if you hold a static wide shot of a street scene for two or three seconds and then suddenly start to zoom in to a close-up of a poster and there is no apparent reason why you started to zoom at that point. It's much better to start the shot at the beginning of the zoom. Or (if you have

remembered the three-for-the-price-of-one technique)
perhaps use the static long shot first and then cut to the
static close-up of the poster. Beware keeping too many
zooms in your film; over-used, they soon become tedious.

wobbly camera   5   As a general rule you shouldn't cut a shot while it is actually
movements   panning or zooming. But with zooms or pans that wobble,
                               try using the static point of the wobble as the beginning of
                               the shot (there is always a static point – often extremely
                               short – where a wobble changes direction). You may also be
                               able to cut early if there is a wobble at the end.

cut on   6   If the shot is moving, don't cut. If a person or thing moves
movement   and you have the action covered by two static shots of
                               different sizes, do cut (if you want to). A person sits down, a
                               car turns into a gate, a telephone is picked up – movements
                               like these disguise cuts most effectively.

don't be hopeful   7   Don't be hopeful about your shots. Some of the shots simply
                               won't be good enough to get into your film and so you
                               should drop them. Don't put them in hoping they are not
                               quite as bad as they look.

mixes (or   8   Few programmes are improved by mixes (also known as
dissolves)   'dissolves'); many look as if they have caught a disease from
                               them. As a general rule use mixes only between sequences,
                               and then only if there is a special reason. Watch well-made
                               programmes and observe how and when mixes have been
                               used in them. Then when you have acquired the 'feel' of
                               mixes, introduce them into your own programmes – but
                               sparingly.

overlaying   9   If you want to overlay an interview with shots illustrating
pictures   what the interviewee is saying, choose the shots for the
                               overlay but don't ask the editor to put them in till you have
                               finished editing. The reason is that if you decide later to
                               shorten the interview the editor has a lot of extra work
                               making the shots fit again. So leave the overlays till the end
                               of the editing period. Interview cutaways should also be
                               left till last for the same reason. Remember also that you
                               don't have to use all the cutaways you have shot – use them
                               only to improve the interview, not just because they are
                               there.

                               Incidentally, when you overlay an interview you have an
                               opportunity to make the sound flow really smoothly. So cut
                               out all 'ums' and 'ers' and repetitions and pauses from the
                               sound track, always bearing in mind that your interviewee's
                               style should remain recognisable, even if it has acquired a
                               strange fluency!

keep everything   10   Don't throw away shots, or even bits of shots, while you are still editing. You never know what you might want to put back into the film. Keep every scrap of film until the editing is finished and approved by your boss; it won't cost extra and might save you a lot of wasted time rummaging about in the waste bin. Bits of shots can also come in useful in surprising ways. I can remember the out-of-focus part of a shot of a surgeon which worked beautifully as the point of view of a patient drifting away under the anaesthetic.

duration   11   Your first assembly should be 10–15 per cent longer than the target duration for the film, and the editing process should slowly reduce this to the length you require. Don't worry about making the film a little shorter than expected if it means you can drop weak and repetitive material. But warn your boss if this is going to happen.

You may have to go through some of the sequences five or six times viewing, cutting, reviewing and recutting before you get them right. Other sequences, equally, may fall into place more easily. But you should never be frightened of working really hard at editing – it's time very well spent. There's a lot of truth in the saying that films are *made* in the cutting room.

When you have finished editing you will probably have to show the programme and read out a first draft of the commentary to someone senior. When the programme has been approved, you should get the commentary ready (see the next step).

laying the commentary as a sound track   It's worth thinking at this stage about recording the commentary wild and having the editor lay it as a separate sound track, as this is the most reliable method of ensuring a really snug fit between words and picture. To do this, you write the commentary in the normal way, show the commentator the programme and then let him record the commentary wild (that is, without having the picture in front of him). The editor then trims the picture and commentary so that they fit each other exactly. But you mustn't let this technique become an excuse for writing the commentary first and then trying to fit the picture to it. The picture must come first.

the final cut   In fact once you have finished editing (and laid the commentary if you are using this method) you should treat this cut as final and not give way to any second thoughts.

The editor still has a lot of work to do splitting the sound track for dubbing, finding and laying extra sound effects, checking the tape joins and so on. If you keep coming back with more ideas about trimming sequences his job becomes impossible. One or two adjustments because of difficulties with the commentary may be entertained. But any more is too much.

Editing Video
The procedure for editing video is different from that for editing film. You will almost certainly be more limited in the amount of time which you can reserve on the video machines, and so will have to think in terms of hours – rather than days or weeks – for editing your programme.

So it is important to make the most of the time you do manage to get on the editing machines. The way to do this is to make a copy of your recorded material on a videocassette and to do all your viewing and planning using this. You should aim to have all your cuts worked out to the last detail **time code** and written down, before you start work on the main tape. If you can arrange to have time code recorded on the cassette and master recording, you should do so. This consists of an electronic counter recorded on the top or bottom of the picture. Make sure that you get the same numbers on both master and copies and you then have a way of identifying all your intended cuts down to the last frame.

If you can't get time code, use the counters provided on the video machine. Some video machines have electronic counters which are as accurate as time code; others have not very accurate mechanical counters using unspecified units which may not match anything on the editing machines. It's worth checking that your viewing and editing machines have identical counters before you start working out your cuts.

Either way you should arrive for your editing session with a written list of all your proposed cuts, specifying each one as precisely as possible by a timing, a short note of the shot and the reason for cutting.

I suggest including a reason for cutting because it's easy to forget why you originally decided – for example – to trim an interview at a particular point. If the cut proves difficult, the editor may ask how vital the trim is. The interviewee might have embarked on a long irrelevant story (in which case the cut is badly needed) or might have just begun to repeat himself (in which case, the cut could be postponed). If you can't remember the reason and don't have a note of it, valuable time will be wasted running through the interview to reassess the cut.

The advent of relatively cheap editing equipment has made it possible to go one better than just viewing and planning your video edit in advance. You can now do your editing in advance on the videocassette to see what it will look like; then when you are satisfied, you cut your high-quality broadcast tapes using the edited cassette as a model.

off-lining

This pre-edit on cassette is known as an **off-line** edit: it's the video equivalent of the film technique of working on a cutting copy first and then when you are satisfied, cutting your master to match. Off-lining has two main advantages. It gives you time (on relatively cheap machines) which you couldn't afford on the high-quality tape-editing machines (which work out very expensive indeed). And it gives you the chance to have second, and third, and fourth thoughts about the best way to use your shots. This isn't usually possible with video, as we shall see.

cutting videotape

In the early days of videotape edits were made by cutting the tape physically and joining it up again (the editors used a microscope, precision guillotine and a special extremely thin sticky tape). Each cut took about ten minutes to do and the joined up tape was not considered fit to be used for another programme afterwards. Not surprisingly this time-consuming and expensive practice was abandoned as soon as a way was found of recording on to a tape without a break between shots and without the picture jumping. So you now have two techniques of editing videotape electronically – the assemble edit and the insert edit.

assemble editing

The assemble edit is really just the process of transferring all the shots that make up your programme on to a blank tape at the right length (remember the natural life-span) and in the right order. You need two machines: one to play back your recorded tapes, the other to record them. Start by transferring your opening shot from the playback to the record tape. When you come to something in the playback tape which you don't want in the finished programme, you ask the videotape editor to stop both machines and then run the playback tape on (or back) to the next shot which you want in the programme.

This shot is then copied from the playback to the record machine with a clean cut from the previous shot. If you wish, the cut between the two shots can be rehearsed so that you can see what the cut will look like without actually recording it. If you are happy with the cut, the editor will then 'print' the shot; the machines will automatically reset themselves, repeat the cut exactly and then continue transferring until the next edit.

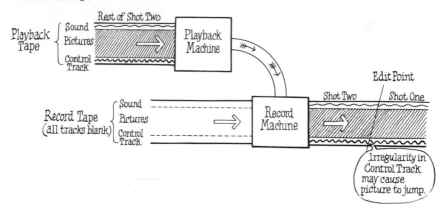

When assembling your programme in this way you obviously have to start at the beginning and work right through the whole programme making your cuts as you go. This is more difficult to do than it sounds. If you have edited film you will know how much impact you can add to the material by swapping a shot round here, trimming a sequence there – you are a sculptor shaping something beautiful out of a formless hunk of rock a chip at a time. But the video editing process requires you to get each cut right before you move on to the next one. It's very unforgiving.

video generations

What happens if you have second thoughts about a sequence in the middle of a twenty-minute programme which you have just finished editing? If you decide to shorten one of the shots you will have to start again from that shot and reassemble all the shots which follow it in the programme. Why not get another tape and copy everything up to the offending cut on to the new tape, trim the shot and then copy everything that follows it? Because you will end up with a copy of a copy of your original shots – a third-generation copy – and the picture quality is likely to be much reduced. Your original shots were first generation, the edited programme is second generation, the copy of the edited programme is third generation. Don't forget that it's likely that you will want to make further copies of your edited programme for keeping in the library, sales to other stations, showing to contributors, and so on. These fourth generation copies will really begin to show their age, especially if they are on the cheaper domestic video systems.

Of course technology can come to the rescue. Digital recording techniques will make it possible to copy and recopy to as many generations as you like without loss of picture quality (because digital systems transfer the specifications for producing the picture, not the picture itself). Or editing machines controlled by computers can repeat automatically all your original edits before and after the change(s) you want to make. In the meantime you have off-line editing which allows you to cut and recut, copy and recopy to as many generations as you wish because you are only building up a model for the final programme.

insert editing

The procedure for the insert edit is exactly the same as for the assemble edit except for one technical difference. With assemble editing the control track is assembled as you go along. With insert editing the control track is laid down on the record tape in advance.

What is the control track? Why should you lay it in advance?

control track

The easiest way to understand the control track and what it does is to think of it as electronic sprocket holes (the holes you see on bits of film). Video machines use the control track (recorded as a continuous signal along the side of the tape) to lock onto and thus ensure that the video head can process the information on the tape correctly and that the tape is running at the right speed. If you lay the control track as you go along in fits and starts (as in assemble editing) it's extremely difficult for the machine to record the control track accurately enough to prevent the picture sometimes jumping at the joins in the track. If on the other hand you lay down the control track in one uninterrupted session before you start editing (make sure you record enough to cover the duration of your completed programme)

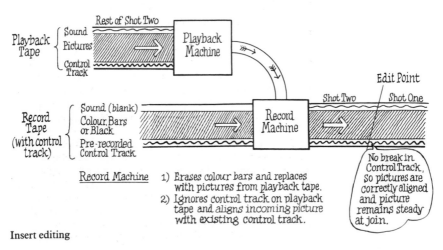

Insert editing

89

the machine has a precise line of electronic sprocket holes which it can use to align the incoming picture during editing. The result is the complete elimination of jumps and flashes in the picture caused by irregularities in the control track. This alone makes it well worth always pre-recording a control track and editing entirely in the insert mode.

editing picture and sound separately

Insert editing offers another advantage as well: the ability to edit picture and sound separately (on some machines this is not possible when assemble editing). Letting the sound overlap a difficult picture cut often helps disguise the cut; it can also help to smooth out an awkward change of pace in the sound track. If you have a programme with a complicated sound track it's best to arrange a special sound dubbing session, just as you would for film. But beware if you transfer the sound track to another machine (video or audio). If the machines aren't running at precisely the same speed you may not be able to get the final mixed sound track back into sync with the pictures.

The other advantage of insert editing is of course that it allows you to do an insert. This means that you can change a shot anywhere in a tape without transferring the whole tape provided that you put in exactly the same length of picture as you took out. The shot you want to put in is lined up against the shot you want to take out by means of cue signals. The two machines are then started together and the recording machine automatically replaces the picture between the cue signals with whatever is in the playback machine at the same moment. It's a straightforward process from the technical point of view, but difficult to get right artistically.

special effects

If you want to use some of the marvellous special effects which video now offers, you should try and arrange a separate time for these before your main editing time. The effects will probably have to be done on a different machine which has to be specially booked. In any case special effects always take longer to do than you thought; it could be disastrous if you ended up using all your normal editing time just working on the effects for one or two sequences.

All the points mentioned in the film editing section (avoiding too many zooms, cutting the first question off interviews and so on) of course apply to video editing as well. For everything except news (where the need for speed makes different standards of editing and picture quality acceptable) your finished programme should be as smooth and polished on video as it is on film.

SUMMARY EIGHTH STEP

Editing Film and Video

Editing is selecting – selecting the best shots for telling your story. Try and find the natural lifespan of each shot.

Editing Film
Check that the editor has received all film and sound rolls.

Wait till all picture and sound have been synchronised before viewing. Commag sound should also be transferred to sepmag for editing (unless it is urgent news film).

View all material with the editor, explaining what it's about. Listen to his comments carefully – he is your first viewer.

Make a shot list.

Give the editor an assembly order (unlikely to be the same as the order in the treatment).

Stay with the editor as much as possible. The cutting room is the best place to learn about making films.

View the first assembly non-stop to assess the overall impact of the programme. Then go through all the sequences three or four times, looking for ways of improving each shot.

Things to look out for:

1 Check that you have found the best possible length for each shot.

2 Are your cuts smooth? Do the points of interest in neighbouring shots fall in the same part of the screen? Jump cuts can often be made to work using this principle. But make sure shot sizes are different – cuts between same size shots of one person or thing are always ugly.

3 Trim the first question from the front of interviews and write its content into the commentary. If possible cut out bits of interview which are merely repetitious or embroidery.

4 Trim the static bits at both ends of pans or zooms. Don't keep too many zooms in the programme.

5 Don't cut in the middle of camera movements. Wobbles in pans or zooms can often be used as cutting points.

6 Do cut when the person or thing in the shot moves (if you want to, and have overlapping shots not the same size).

7 Drop poor shots. Don't hope they might be better than they look. They won't.

8 Use mixes (dissolves) very sparingly.

9 Let the editor put in overlay shots and interview cutaways last. Remember to cut out all 'ums' and 'ers' from overlaid sound.

10 Keep all rejected shots until editing is finished. Throw nothing away.

11 Slowly reduce film to the duration required. Don't worry about it being a bit short. But warn your boss if it is.

Get the film and draft commentary approved.

For a really snug fit between words and pictures finalise commentary, record it wild and have the editor lay it as a separate sound track.

Once cut is final, only ask for vital changes.

Editing Video

Video editing time is limited. So make full use of what time you do get on editing machines by

– making a videocassette recording of your material and working out all your cuts on this in advance using time code if available

– arriving at the editing session with a written list of proposed cuts identifying each with a number, shot description and reason for the cut

– off-line editing when possible

– completing special effects sequences before the main editing session.

There are two types of video editing:

– assemble editing, which is transferring all the bits making up the programme in order on to a completely blank tape.

– insert editing, which is transferring the programme to a tape with a prerecorded control track.

Use insert editing whenever possible.

Commentary Writing

Commentary writing should always be at the back of your mind while you are editing your programme. Although you are concentrating on the picture and sound, it's helpful to keep a list of possible commentary points for each sequence as you go along, so that by the time you finish editing you have an outline commentary down on paper.

You should then consider if your points are in the places where they will have the maximum impact. If for example you are doing a story about a man who is helping poor villagers improve their standard of living, the fact that the man is himself the son of a poor villager may be an interesting thing to mention at the beginning of the story, or it may have more impact if mentioned at the end. Obviously the position of the fact is important: don't waste your chance of making the most of it. Pictures may be more important than words while you are editing, but you must not underestimate the power of words; if chosen carefully, words can determine and even change the viewer's attitude to what he sees. The picture of the tanker on the horizon can either be an attractive seascape or an example of pollution – it all depends what you say about it in the commentary.

There are two important points about commentary writing – one is a DO and one is a DON'T.

DO make the commentary fit the picture.
DON'T describe what you can see in the picture.

don't describe

Let's take the DON'T first. Nothing sounds worse than telling the viewer what he can see in the picture for himself. Take, for example, a line like 'the General steps out of the helicopter and greets the people waiting to meet him'. The viewer can presumably see all that for himself. But he can't work out from the picture what the names and the jobs of the waiting people are, the type of helicopter and its performance, the significance of the General's visit, and so on. So don't just describe the picture but add to it; give it extra meaning with your words.

do make the commentary fit

Now for the DO. Do make the commentary fit the picture. The way to ensure this is to make a shot list of the edited programme, taking special note of the shots over which you will need commentary. Put the picture on the left and notes about the sound on the right. You can count in feet or minutes and seconds, whichever scale is used on your editing machines and in your station's dubbing theatre.* Here is an example of a shot list:

timing	picture	sound
0	LS farm dogs chasing decoy hares	SOVT** (recorded effects)
47½ secs	CU Bert	Commentary: introduce Bert and his hobby
1' 17"	CU scar on hand	
1' 33"	Bert interview	SOVT 'Nothing better . . . . . . make her a winner'
3' 05"	crowd in stadium	Commentary: the big night of the race
3' 30"	the race	no commentary, just sound effects and stadium commentator
	etc.	etc.

*There are two types of film feet in use: 35 mm feet and 16 mm feet. 35 mm film is larger and therefore passes through cameras, projectors and so on more quickly; so there are more 35 mm feet per minute than 16 mm feet per minute. This means that 35 mm feet are a more precise way of labelling film – simply because there are more numbers per minute. For this reason (and to avoid confusion with 16 mm feet) most organisations like the BBC use 35 mm feet for all their films, even their 16 mm films. It's a sensible policy.

**SOVT = sound on videotape

This shot list contains enough detail for the commentary which I intend to write. The long shot of the farm at the beginning of the programme and the pictures of the greyhounds chasing mechanical (or decoy) hares don't need any commentary and so I have not bothered to go into any detail about them in the shot list. Bert is the main character in the film and so needs some introduction when he appears at 47½ seconds. I want to draw attention to a scar on his hand and so have noted the timing for this. His introduction will continue (in short passages) till 1 minute 33 seconds when Bert starts talking in his sync interview. I have noted the first and last words of this part of his interview to remind me of what he said and also because it might be neat to pick up some of his spoken words in the commentary. Then there are 25 seconds from 3 min 05 to 3 min 30 to set the scene at the greyhound racing stadium for the race in which one of Bert's dogs is running . . ..

And so on.

do your own shot list

This shot list notes all the points I will want for my commentary: timings, details of some shots, and the first and last words of interviews. The important thing, however, is that these are the points which **I** want to bring out in my commentary. Another scriptwriter may see different things in the picture which he wants to comment on (the size of the farm or the decoy hares for example), and so his shot list will be slightly different. The point to note therefore is this: always do your own shot list. No one else can see the film through your eyes.

write first, check against picture later

One you have your shot list, go somewhere quiet to write the commentary. Some people like to skip doing a shot list and try and write their commentary in front of a playback machine, checking each sentence against the tape as soon as they have written it. This may suit some people. For most, however, repeatedly running the pictures backwards and forwards is merely a distraction when you should be concentrating on the words. Far better to work hard on getting the words right first (and it is hard work). Then check against the picture later.

How do you make the commentary fit the picture? The answer is: you count.

counting words

Find out from someone experienced how many words per foot or per second of programme you should allow in your language. (With English the usual ratio is 2½ to 3 words per second, depending on where you are – different countries speak and understand English at different speeds.) Then write each bit of commentary, counting the number of words and adding or dropping words till the passage fits its allotted length of picture exactly. If you find it a nuisance to count words while you are writing, it's a useful tip to write on square paper

with	a	ration	of	say	six
words	per	line	with	the	words
set	out	in	vertical	columns	like
this.	In	this	way	you	can
tell	at	a	glance	that	assuming
your	commentator	speaks	at	three	words
a	second,	you	have	written	enough
for	sixteen	seconds	of	film.	

don't use a stopwatch

Alternatively, you can use an ordinary piece of lined paper with columns folded into it. Whatever you do, don't use a stopwatch to work out how long each bit of commentary will run. The reason is that it is almost impossible to read the commentary to yourself at the speed your commentator will read in the dubbing theatre and so your stopwatch timings will almost certainly be wrong.

The first passage of commentary (each passage is usually referred to as a 'cue') should not be earlier than 3 seconds (or 5 feet) into the programme to reduce the risk of any words being lost if the front of the programme is clipped off by mistake during transmission. If you want part of the commentary in the middle of a cue to coincide with a particular shot, you should note the timing of this shot in

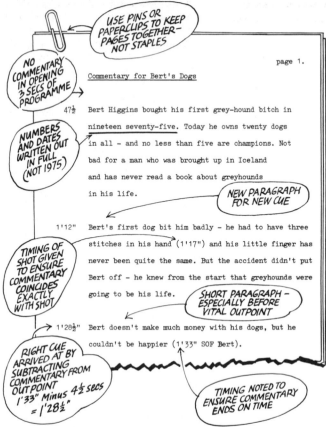

brackets at the appropriate point (see illustration above). The same goes for commentary which must be finished by a certain point (see the last cue in the illustration). These sorts of cues should be worked out by counting backwards from the crucial word(s). They should also be kept short, as the longer the lead-in, the more chance there is that a slight variation in reading speed will make the commentary fall short of – or spill over into – the next shot.

In fact all your cues should be kept short. If you are writing more than three or four sentences for a cue, something is wrong. You'll probably find that the picture is communicating very little and you are trying to say too much. If this is so, cut the number of ideas as well as the number of words. Also cut the picture (if it's not too late) so that your programme moves more rapidly on to the next sequence. The best television commentary is simple, clear and brief.*

*There's more about the art of commentary writing in Briefing No. 16

script lay-out

The finished commentary should be typed out on paper which doesn't make a noise when handled. The last cue on each page should not run over on to the next page; if the complete cue won't fit, start it on the next page. It's better also to pin or paperclip the pages together rather than staple them: this makes it easier for the reader to handle each page separately and thus avoid rustling the paper when he starts a new page. It also helps the reader if all numbers and dates are written out in words as in the illustration.

Finally, don't cover everything with commentary. Leave room for the interviews, music and sound effects – and also for your viewers to draw breath. When you've finished writing and counting, read the commentary out loud to yourself to take out the flaws (which when you say it aloud sounds more like a job for a builder than a writer and should therefore be replaced with something clearer). And then check the commentary against the picture before you go to the dubbing theatre: it should be a perfect fit, but things have been known to go wrong.

SUMMARY

Commentary Writing

Keep a list of commentary points for each sequence during editing. Check important facts are put where they have most impact.

DON'T describe what the viewer can see for himself in the picture.

DO make the commentary fit the picture

– by doing your own shot list

– by writing the commentary first and checking later

– by counting words per foot or second

– by not using a stop-watch to time each passage.

Don't start the first cue earlier than three seconds (or five feet) into the programme.

Note the places where the commentary must fit exactly by putting the timings in brackets on the script. Keep cues leading up to these points short.

Keep cues in general short. The best television commentary is simple, clear and brief.

Don't let cues run over to the next page.

Use pins or paperclips, not staples, to keep pages together.

Write out all numbers in words.

Don't cover everything with commentary. Leave the viewer room to breathe.

Check commentary by reading it out loud to yourself (take out the flaws!)

Check the commentary against the picture before dubbing.

Dubbing Theatre

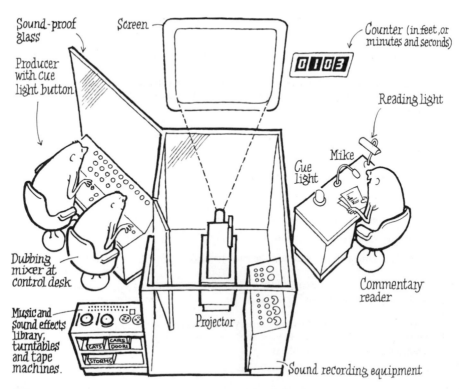

Sound-proof glass

Screen

Counter (in feet, or minutes and seconds)

Producer with cue light button

Reading light

Mike

Cue Light

Dubbing mixer at control desk

Commentary reader

Music and sound effects library, turntables and tape machines.

CATS DOORS CARS STORMS

Projector

Sound recording equipment

Dubbing Commentary

It's difficult to write much that is useful about dubbing as practices vary so much in different TV stations. A few stations have fully equipped dubbing theatres with a library of music and sound effects; others use the studio to transfer film to videotape, adding commentary and a few sound effects on the way; and yet others smother all parts of the programme which don't have speech on them with soapy music and read the commentary live during transmission.

San Totta of course employs the last method. The commentary and the soapy music quite often run into the recorded speech and it's not unknown for the programme to finish long before the commentator.

The safest way of making sure that the commentary fits the programme is of course to record it wild and dub it on while editing (or lay it if you are using film). Then when you get to the dubbing theatre or studio you have one less thing to worry about.

cueing

If you haven't already recorded your commentary it's usual to start the dubbing session by doing so. Do a rehearsal before you start recording. The reader takes his cues from a green light (the 'cue-light') which is operated by the producer. The cues should always be given half a second (or one foot) before the actual timing in the script, so as to give the commentator time to draw breath and start (no one can do it instantaneously).

'rock and roll'

When you have dealt with any problems thrown up by the rehearsal, record the commentary. If the dubbing theatre is a modern one, you will be able to stop at any point you wish, return to the last cue and begin to record again from there (this system is often known as 'rock and roll'). If the dubbing theatre is an old one or you are recording in a studio, you may not be able to pick up the recording in the middle but may have to go back to the beginning each time that you stop. By the way, if you are using a rock and roll system or recording the commentary wild, it's often worth going back to the first page of the script at the end of the session and recording it again. The first page is usually the most difficult and is much easier for commentators to tackle when their voice has settled down and is relaxed.

the dubbing chart

After the commentary the dubbing mixer (who is the technician in charge) will start work on building up the

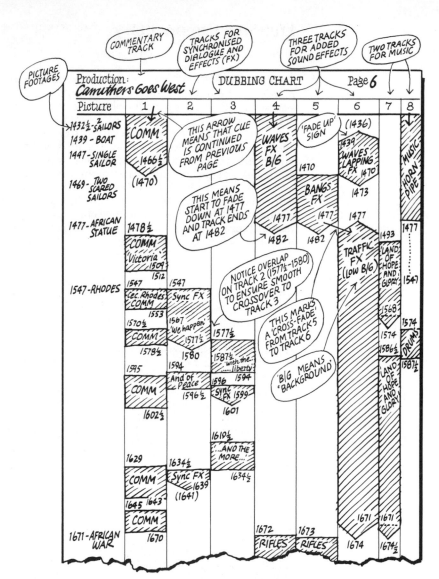

Dubbing Chart
Notice the care and detail
needed to produce a first-
class sound track

music and effects track (also known as the M & E or
International Sound Track). The film editor will have
prepared a dubbing chart listing the exact timings for the
'ins' and 'outs' of all commentary, music, dialogue and
effects (each will have at least one track to itself); the
dubbing mixer will work from this chart to combine all the

different components into one M & E. Your job while this is going on is to make sure that the relative levels of all this sound are recorded as you want them.

When the M & E is ready, the mixer will run through the programme one last time to combine the M & E with the commentary. This is called the Final Mix and you should once again pay attention to the relative levels of the music, effects and speech. Allow for the fact that the speakers in dubbing theatres are usually far better quality than the speakers built into home television sets. As a result sound effects which can be heard clearly but softly in the dubbing theatre may be completely inaudible to the viewer at home; if you suspect this might be happening, discuss it with the dubbing mixer and ask him not to keep the effects too low. Dubbing mixers are often so used to their high-quality speakers and have such finely tuned ears that they forget about the relative insensitivity of viewers' speakers (and ears).

adding sound effects

It's worth paying close attention to what's going on in the dubbing theatre, as a good dub can add a lot of polish to a programme. Carefully chosen sound effects can in a flash create an atmosphere which gives the viewer that exciting feeling of being there himself. Dull shots can be brought to life by adding a distant dog bark, bird song, insects buzzing or the sound of wind blowing through the trees. The fit between commentary and the beginning of an interview can often be improved by moving the commentary track forward or backward a fraction (if it wasn't exactly right on the recording). You can give a picture depth by letting the viewer actually hear something from that ship you can see on the horizon. The touches you add may seem tiny and the viewers may not even notice them consciously, but they are still worth making because all these tiny points contribute towards the total impact of the programme.

dubbing in the studio

If you are using the studio to dub or transmit your programme and therefore haven't prepared a formal dubbing chart, it's important that your commentary script should include all the things you intend to do and a stop-watch timing for each of them. For example:

49″	Super title
1′ 23″	Go grams 'Marches' Side 2 Band 3
1′ 54″	Lose grams
3′ 15″	Run tape – birdsong
3′ 55″	Lose tape
7′ 06″	Super caption: General Hiro

These instructions can be written into the commentary script, or if the script is already a long one it might be more convenient for them to be written on a separate sheet for distribution to the vision mixer, floor manager, technical manager, sound supervisor and videotape and telecine operators. The floor manager and sound supervisor will definitely need a copy of the commentary; the other technicians probably won't if they have a copy of the instructions. You should do a full rehearsal before recording so that everyone knows exactly what to do.

sound effects

A word about music and sound effects to end this chapter. Sound effects should be the normal accompaniment to your pictures; I have already stressed the importance of recording and editing them in sync. Without them the impact of your pictures is halved: imagine, for example, the arrival of a helicopter first without sound, and then with it. A well-recorded sound effect can give the beginning of a sequence an enormous boost if it's played loud and left free of commentary. It can also be used to bring drawings or still photographs to life. Mixed with music or taking over after a sequence with music it can be quite magical.

music

Music is also something to conjure with. It has this marvellous power to get through to people's feelings in a few seconds. But you must use it sensitively; don't, for example, cut it abruptly in full flow just because the sequence has ended (fade it out gently instead). Use it like commentary (and sometimes instead of commentary) to add meaning to the picture: a love song played over the shot of a naval vessel leaving its home port can say far more about the feelings of the sailors and the families waving them goodbye than the best written commentary. You can also use music ironically: for example the wedding march played over a scene in a divorce court. And of course you can cut your picture to music as well (so that the cuts coincide with the beat).

When you want to use music as commentary, it's a good idea to drop a hint in the commentary leading up to the music section so that the viewers know what to expect. There are many ways of doing this: a line like 'It's a time for private thoughts' would do for both the examples above.

Whatever you do, don't use music as 'audible chewing-gum'. The music you use must have a definite flavour to communicate to the viewers. So having it gently playing in the background to hide an absence of sound effects, or simply because you think the sound track is a bit quiet, is a terrible waste. If, for example, you have a person in a studio telling a children's story illustrated by drawings, it's perfectly acceptable to have the narrator's voice on the sound track and nothing else. If you think that music would help the story, that's fine too, but don't therefore just play one piece the whole way through. Instead look for the exact points where music would help and play specific bits of music to add meaning to the pictures at these points, perhaps where a character feels sleepy, or is excited, or is in danger.

SUMMARY

Dubbing Commentary

Procedure in the dubbing theatre

1 First rehearse, then record the commentary.
The commentator takes his cue from the green light, not from the timing or footage counter. Remember to cue him a little early each time.

2 Build up and record the M & E (or International Sound Track).

3 Do the final mix (of commentary plus M & E).
Make sure the music and sound effects are not held too low. Look out for chances to use sound effects to bring shots to life.

If dubbing in studio

1 Prepare a sheet listing everything you want to do (or write it into the commentary script). Distribute to those involved.

2 First rehearse, then record.

Sound effects should normally accompany all pictures – without them the impact of pictures is halved.

Never use music as 'audible chewing-gum'; it's far too powerful to waste on covering up the absence of proper sound effects. Use it like commentary to add meaning to pictures.

Studio Programmes

The studio at San Totta TV is the heart of the station. It is also the place where most of the producers come closest to heart failure.

Studios can frighten the inexperienced producer as much as they frighten interviewees. Rows of glaring lights hanging from the ceiling (journalists for some reason often mistake these for cameras), thick padded doors and walls, anything from two to five cameras looking hungrily for something to shoot, a flock of technicians waiting behind double-thickness glass (bullet-proof perhaps?) for the producer's every word (and mistake) – all this could just as well be a torture chamber as a television studio.

Of course the studio need not be a torture chamber. In fact once you know how to do it, directing a studio can become addictive, an exhilarating drug which can stimulate you to a 'high' it takes hours to come down from.

To cut the torture from your time in the studio you have to remember one vital fact: nothing happens in the studio unless you arrange it to happen. So you the producer are – or should be – in total control of what goes on. You have to think of and arrange for everything from the colour of the walls to each step the people in the programme take.

Happily you don't have to do this all by yourself. The various technical departments are there to help and advise. But the main push behind it all has to come from you.

The first thing is to decide what you want in your programme. That's what the earlier chapters in this book are about and any studio producer who has turned to this chapter first, hoping to save himself some reading, would be well-advised to turn back. Ideas, research and treatments are as important for studio programmes as for any other. It's only when you have decided on the contents of your programme that the procedure is different.

book a studio early

Book yourself into a studio as early as possible, in fact as soon as you are sure that you have a programme worth doing. Totta producers tend to treat the studios as casually as the canteen, and drop in when they feel like it; you should approach the studio as carefully as a parent who orders a wedding feast, worrying about each detail of the decor, menu, music and cost.

the 'set'

It makes sense to start with the items which take the longest to prepare. This almost always means the scenery or 'set'. So start by going to your designer and telling him about your programme (what it's trying to achieve, how many artists are involved and what they will do, how big your budget for design is, and so on) and also what sort of set you are thinking of. So – what should you look for in a set?

It's difficult to advise about this since the set depends totally on the type of programme. But if you find yourself asking for a massive complicated set full of the sort of features which are in the houses and countryside all around you, be careful. Perhaps you shouldn't be doing your programme in the studio at all. Wouldn't you be better off on location?

Don't forget the virtues of a simple set brought to life by effective lighting and one or two carefully chosen props. A few rostra (platforms) to break up the flat expanse of the studio floor and a few patches of colour or pattern can work wonders. Remember TV is most at home with mid-shots and close-ups and the chances are that the viewers therefore won't see all that much of the set. Anyway what the people on the set are saying and doing should be holding the viewers' attention more than the set itself. But don't go too far the other way: if a set is too skimped and shoddy it draws attention to itself and away from the people in it, and that of course defeats its purpose.

the floor plan

Use a protractor on the floor plan to check your shots will work.

The designer will need some time to work on his ideas. He will draw them on a floor plan (this is a printed diagram of the studio marked with a grid which you can use to pinpoint any position on the floor). When you receive the design, run through your programme on your mental TV, seeing it in the set and thinking about where your cameras will be, what the cameras will see, where people will stand and sit, where they will come in and where they will go out. Do this systematically from the beginning to the end of the programme and pencil in all the main positions on the floor plan, checking that there is enough room for the cameras to move and that their cables won't become entangled, that floor monitors can be seen by presenters, and so on. It's also worth checking the shots each camera will get with a protractor to make sure that an intended two-shot won't shoot off the edge of the set or that a camera can get far back enough to get everything into the long shot you are planning. You will probably find several problems for you and the designer to solve (better now than in the studio).

Building the set can take anything from a few days to a few weeks. If you add this on to the time needed to design it, you

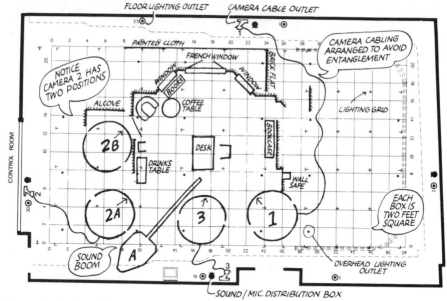

Floor plan for a small 3 camera studio.

can see that you should start work on the set anything from four to six weeks before studio day. One thing is certain: no one ever complains that you are telling them what you want too early – unless of course you start approaching people before you are clear in your own mind what you want. That wastes everybody's time.

If you need special costumes or props you should also talk to the people responsible for these as early as possible.

the planning meeting
The next important date is the planning meeting. This can be a few weeks before your studio day – or only a few days before, if you have a regular weekly programme. The planning meeting is usually attended by the designer and senior members of the studio technical crew who will be on duty on the day of your programme – the technical manager, the lighting supervisor and the sound supervisor. It might be useful to have the floor manager and a representative from the workshop there as well. You should bring to this meeting the floor plan marked with the camera positions and all positions and movements of everyone in the programme. You should also have the contents of your programme written down in note form if the final script isn't ready yet. If you can send those concerned the script (or an outline) a few days beforehand, so much the better.

The best way to conduct a planning meeting is to start by giving a quick outline of the programme and asking the designer to explain the main points of the set. Then run through the programme explaining all the movements, positions and actions of the participants and cameras at each stage. The technicians won't want you to read the script to them, but they will want to know things like – where is the presenter at the beginning of the programme? Is he standing or sitting? Is he in position when the programme starts or does he walk in? If he walks in – where does he walk in from? Which camera will he be looking at? And so on. All these details are vital to your technicians. Without them they cannot give you the lighting, sound and pictures you want.

the camera script

The next stage after the planning meeting is to finish the script, if you haven't already done so. This should then be typed out in the form of a camera script, containing not only everything which will be said in the programme but also all the details of shots, camera movements, sound coverage and so on. You should keep to the layout normally used in your studios if it differs from the one shown in the illustration, as the important thing about the script is that everyone should understand it.

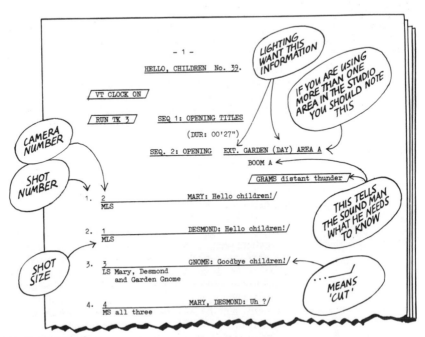

Camera Script example

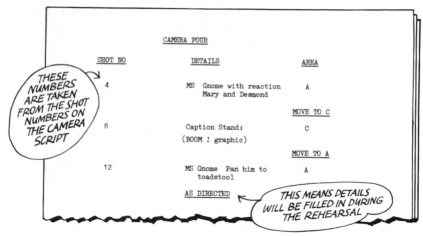

Camera Card example

camera cards

When the script is finished the next job is to prepare camera cards. These are cards given to each cameraman listing all his shots; they are in fact individual scripts for each camera. It is best to have them typed out with lots of space between each shot so that the cameramen can make their own notes during the rehearsal.

running order

For news and current affairs programmes it isn't usually possible to prepare a detailed camera script and camera cards in advance – too much of the programme is unscripted, items are added or dropped or come in late. For this sort of programme it's best to put each item on a separate page, noting the title of the item, introductory words in full, the opening and closing words of any inserts from videotape or film, and actual or intended durations. Often items recorded in advance are given alternative out cues so that adjustments can be made during transmission to make sure the programme doesn't overrun. The pages for all the items are then assembled and a running order put at the front. The layout of this sort of script makes it easy to add late items or drop others (just add or drop pages).

The closer you get to the day of your studio booking, the more there seems to do. You have to check that everyone and everything involved with the programme is briefed, ordered, correct and knows where and when to arrive. Don't forget to ask your participants to come early if they need special make-up, or if there are a lot of them needing make-up (in both cases you should warn the make-up department). Graphics, props, costumes, music, sound effects – everything needs to be checked by you personally.

PLUG (Programme One)

THIS MEANS CAMERA 2 IN POSITION A CAMERA 3 IN POSITION B

CUMULATIVE TOTALS AFTER EACH ITEM IN THIS COLUMN

RUNNING ORDER

THESE ITEMS ARE PRE-RECORDED

SEQUENCE	ITEM	PRESENTER	CAMERAS	SOUND	Estimated DURATION	Overall DURATION
1	TITLES Opening Link	 Di	VT 2A	SOVT	46" 15"	46" 1'01"
2	VIBES SONG 'Nook'		VT	SOVT	2'34"	3'35"
3	M. BIBER INTERVIEW	Roger	1A 2B 3A		3'00"	6'35"
4	...AL DEMO	Di	2A 3B		3'30"	10'05"
5	TV STROBES DANCE		1A 2B	GRAMS	2'25"	12'30"
6	FIRST NIGHT REVIEWS	Di Roger	1B 2A 3B		4'30"	17'00"
7	HIT SONG		VT	SOVT	1'45"	18'45"
8	PLUGS RECAP	Di Roger	1B 2A 3B		4'00"	22'45"
9	CLOSING	Di Roger	1B		15"	23'00"

Running Order example

Time passes very quickly on the day itself and there are always a few emergencies which you can't foresee (like camera breakdowns) which will eat into your rehearsal time. So make sure as many snags as possible are sorted out in advance: the more things you know are right, the more time you have for coping with the problems you can't foresee.

is the set clean?

Then comes the great day itself – studio day. Make sure you arrive at least half an hour early to give yourself time to talk to the technicians and familiarise yourself with the position of everything in relation to your floor plan. Then check the set itself. Is it clean and freshly painted? Has it been damaged or marked while being put up? If the set is regularly used, is it showing any signs of wear and tear (usually noticeable at the edges)? Are the cables in the back of the set out of sight? Are there any cigarette stubs, sweet wrappings or chalk marks from the last programme on the floor? If you find any of these, speak to your designer about it. The studio camera can't turn a blind eye to a grubby set and nor should you.

When it's time to begin your rehearsal ask the technical manager if everything is ready. If it is, get down to work without delay.

the run-through

Start by doing a run-through of the programme, shot by shot. Take each shot in turn, look at it, confirm to the cameraman that it's what you want or ask him to zoom in or out, pan right or left, or whatever. When you are satisfied with the shot, tell the cameraman. Then move on to the next shot and do the same again. This shot-by-shot run-through should never be skipped. It's the only chance you have of telling the cameraman exactly what you want from each shot; if you don't do it, the cameramen are in effect reduced to guessing your intentions from the notes on their camera cards.

When you have lined up the shots for a tricky sequence – one with lots of captions, for example – stop the run-through and try and put the sequence together. It helps break the ice in the studio. Everybody concentrates to get the sequence right and when it is almost right (it doesn't have to be perfect at this stage) it's reassuring for everyone to know that that bit works and that they can function effectively as a team. It's worth putting a sequence together like this early in your rehearsal time.

The run-through may show up all sorts of problems, some of which you may have to get round by adding or dropping shots. Announce any shot changes clearly on the talk-back.

adding shots

New shots should be given the number of the previous shot followed by a letter – 'Add shot 27A – camera 3 – close-up: presenter's hands'. Give everyone time to note the change on their scripts.

By the way, this first run-through can be started before the set and lighting are completely ready: there's no point holding things up because a table or flower-pot hasn't been put into position. You also don't need to wait until all your participants have arrived – you can always line up your shots using someone else as a stand-in. But make sure your stand-ins are about the same height and size as your participants – this is important for lighting as well as cameras.

After the first run-through rehearse any tricky bits which you didn't stop for the first time. View the beginnings and ends of any videotape or film inserts (if you don't have time to view the whole insert) to make sure everyone knows the best place to cut to and away from them. Then go through the whole programme again, but this time try to do it at the correct speed. If you have any time left after this second run-through, use it to rehearse again the sections where things went wrong.

All too soon you will find that you have to stop rehearsing because it's time for 'line-up'. The engineers need this time (usually it's half an hour) to check the cameras and the rest of the equipment; your participants can use it to rest and have their make-up refreshed. And you can use it for last-minute instructions to the participants. But please, only a few instructions as this is not time to start major changes in the programme.

*See Briefing No. 1 for what to say when directing in the studio

Then you start transmitting or recording the programme. If you have prepared and rehearsed well, you should need to say* very little while this is going on beyond giving instructions to the vision mixer. Instead you should concentrate always on keeping one jump ahead of the programme, checking that the next shot is ready, that the next graphic is in place, that the next participant is standing by. In particular make sure the shot you're cutting to isn't the same size as the shot you are on. If it is, change the size of the waiting shot – or don't cut. Don't relax during the recorded inserts; use the time to check that everything is ready for the next section of the programme.

Good luck!

Here are some further points about studio programmes.

1 *Sound at the Opening*
At the beginning of a programme it looks much neater if you bring up the sound a tiny bit before the picture; bringing up the picture first gives the impression that the sound department is asleep. Bringing up the sound first doesn't for some reason make the picture department look bad, perhaps because it doesn't feel as if the programme has really started until you see the picture. Anyway, whatever the reason, sound should lead.

2 *Cut-off Monitors*
Viewers at home will see slightly less of the picture than you can see in the studio. This is not because their screen is smaller, but because most home television sets are tuned to make the picture look as large as possible, even though this means losing a strip all the way round the edge of it (engineers say these sets are 'overscanned'). So make sure

Cut-off

that important bits of information are not too near the edge of the screen. Words in particular can easily lose a letter or two if you aren't careful. If you ask, the technical manager can show you the extent of the cut-off on the preview monitor.

3   *Preview Monitor*
Don't forget the preview monitor. In most studios the monitors for each of the cameras are black and white, with only the transmission monitor (often labelled 'TX' for short) and the preview monitor in colour. You can ask for any picture from the other monitors to be shown on the preview monitor. This gives you a chance to see if any colours are clashing; or to check how a name caption, for example, will look when superimposed over a shot of an interviewee whose knees are showing at the bottom of the picture – it's usually better to tighten the shot so the caption misses the knees.

4   *Small Studios*
Don't be put off if you have only two cameras (or even one) at your disposal. After all, when you are on location you will have only one camera to work with 99 per cent of the time. In studio programmes where you can't stop between every shot, one camera only is of course limiting (try recording in chunks and using caption scanners and pre-recorded inserts to give variety). If you plan carefully, two cameras are adequate for all but the most complicated programmes. Here again you can work wonders by pre-recording complicated bits of the programme and playing them in.

5   *Studio Marvels*
Even the most unambitious studio has a surprising number of technical tricks built into it. Most of them are hardly ever used because producers simply don't know they are there. So take time one day (not on your studio day of course) to ask a friendly engineer to show you what the studio can do; electronic colours, fancy wipes, black and coloured edging, cut-outs, electronic letters, numbers and arrows, chromakey, flashing coloured lights, different lenses and filters, sound echoes, reverse phasing and so on. You'll be surprised how many effects are available.

6   *Vision Mixing*
Some producers seem to think that this is a relatively unskilled job which they can handle themselves. Don't be one of them. By now you should have realised that you have more than enough to do without worrying about working all the controls as well. The argument is sometimes heard that because the vision mixer is waiting for your cue he is always

a fraction behind. The reply to this is that a good vision mixer will foresee your intention and will therefore cut almost instantaneously; in any case you should, like the conductor of an orchestra, always be giving your cues a fraction before you want him to act on them.

7 *Studio Crews*
Remember that crews are made up of human beings. So telling them who you are at the beginning (they may not recognise your voice over the talk-back even if they have met you), an occasional 'please' and 'thank you' and a ten-minute break for refreshments are all appreciated. Be alert, enthusiastic and calm when you direct; show concern for other people's problems and don't lose your sense of humour. Above all, don't snap your fingers when cutting – every snap loses you another friend.

8 *Studio Discipline*
If you have problems with members of the crew (the sound supervisor, perhaps, doesn't seem to be listening to your instructions, the lighting men are having a loud conversation which is disturbing your concentration), don't try and solve them yourself. Ask the technical manager to speak to the crew; he is their direct boss.

If observers in the gallery are making a noise it's up to you the director to ask them to be quiet (should they be there at all?). If your boss is in the gallery and like Magnus Vision, Totta's General Manager, makes a habit of interrupting with suggestions at crucial moments, ask him to keep them for a convenient break in the rehearsal. If (like Mr Vision) he still keeps on interrupting, there comes a point when you have to consider giving him your chair and asking him to direct the programme . . . but this of course is a drastic step. Mr Vision fancies himself as a sportsman and so often turns up in the studio for Caesar Andante's 'Sports Round-Up'. One day when Mr Vision had made one too many suggestions Caesar turned round and asked him to take over the programme. Pause, while everybody waited to see what the GM would do. 'No,' said he, 'you carry on, Andante; if I did it, the change of style would be much too noticeable.'

Not for nothing is Magnus Vision the General Manager of San TTV.

But he stopped making suggestions after this, and a little later went out of the studio. So Caesar had made his point.

9 *Breakdowns*
If the studio isn't ready on time to start the rehearsal and

Make a discreet note of
time lost because of
technical breakdowns

there are also technical breakdowns which eat into your
precious time, it's useful to make a discreet note of how long
you have lost as the result of each incident. You are not
entitled to have this time made up to you as a right (you
have to expect to lose some time for breakdowns). But as it is
not unknown for technicians to say the programme got into
difficulties because the producer wasn't properly prepared,
it's just as well to have a few facts available on your side of
the argument.

SUMMARY

Studio Programmes

In the studio you have total control over what goes on. So
nothing happens unless you arrange it.

Make sure that the studio is booked for your use on the right
day at the right time.

Get design and construction departments working on your
set as early as possible. Visualise your programme in the set
to identify problems before the design goes off to be built.

Order costumes and props early.

Invite the designer, technical manager and sound and
lighting supervisors to the planning meeting. Bring the floor
plan with positions for the cameras and participants marked
on it. Run through the programmes explaining all the
positions and movements.

Finalise the camera script and prepare camera cards.

Check everything and everyone in the programme personally as studio day approaches. Do they know where and when to come? Allow time for make-up when telling participants what time they should turn up. Everything you can get right in advance, you should; this will leave you with more time to cope with the unforeseeable snags.

On studio day arrive at least half an hour early. Check the set for cleanliness.

Do a shot-by-shot run-through first, telling the technicians how you want each shot. Rehearse tricky sections. View all programme inserts.

Then go through the programme again at correct speed. Make a note of any outstanding problems and use the remaining time to eliminate them.

During 'line-up' you can talk to your participants about the programme, but please leave time for resting and touching-up make-up.

Don't try to make changes during the transmission or recording. Instead, concentrate on cueing the vision mixer and keeping one jump ahead in the programme to make sure everything is right.

Further Points

1   For a sound opening sound should lead.

2   Allow for cut-off in home television sets when framing shots.

3   Use the preview monitor to check colours and the position of superimpositions.

4   All but the most complicated programmes can be successfully made using only two cameras if you plan carefully and use pre-recorded inserts from VT.

5   Arrange a demonstration of all studio marvels.

6   Don't do your own vision mixing.

7   Technicians are humans. Treat them accordingly.

8   Studio discipline: let the technical manager look after the crew. You look after the rest.

9   Keep a discreet note of time lost through technical breakdowns.

Outside Broadcasts

Outside broadcasts are the reverse of studio programmes. With studio programmes you put the location in the studio; with outside broadcasts you put the studio in the location.

Because that is what a traditional OB unit is: a studio on wheels complete with camera, vision mixing desk, sound and videotape machines, talkback and a graphics generator. Everything that is found in the standard studio except for those rows of lights hanging from the roof (and if anyone could think of a cheap way of hanging them from the sky, they would also come in handy).

It follows therefore that to do an OB you use a mixture of location filming and studio programme techniques. The main thing you borrow from your location technique is the recce (refresh your memory of the Recce chapter). But with a first-time OB in a new location the recce is not just advisable – it's essential. Even if the location is one you've used before, you should go back for a survey. Things could have changed, and you may have to change your plans.

the OB recce

The OB engineer must come along with you on the recce. The traditional, full-scale OB unit needs a great deal of technical support and the engineer is the one who has to organise it: a nearby source of mains electricity (or a mobile generator), telephone lines and microwave links back to the studio (if you're transmitting the programme live), raised platforms for the camera if you want them to look down on the action (and you almost certainly do), slings and gantries to get the cable across the roads without obstructing traffic, approval from local safety officers about any structures you build, and so on. If you are taking a large OB to a remote area the engineer may even have to check the strength of the bridges on the way: full-size OB units need support below the ground as well as above it. Of course if you have one of the new light-weight OB units (which are really just portable video cameras in a specially designed back-up vehicle) you won't have to worry about things like bridges, but a lot of other points about OB planning will still apply.

On the recce the engineer will first want to know the basic details of the programme: the nature, time and duration of the event, the location of prize-giving ceremonies, interviews and any other action.

camera positions

The thing to decide then is the position of the cameras.

Traditional cameras are a lot less mobile than light-weight ones, and so once you have picked camera positions you probably won't be able to change them. And of course these camera positions are extremely important – for you, because the success of your shots depends on them; for the engineer, because he probably has only a limited length of cabling and will have to juggle around with the placing of the OB van to give you the positions you ask for.

The engineer will also want to know which lenses you want on which camera; there is usually a selection of wide-angle and short or long zoom lenses on offer. You should ask the engineer's advice if you find it difficult to decide what should go where on your first OB. You may also have one or more remote cameras available (cameras which don't need to be connected up to the OB van with cables). These are obviously useful to cover areas which you can't reach with cabled cameras, or areas where you want shots from lots of different angles (which you won't be able to get from a fixed camera).

So where should you put your cameras? The following notes will give you a rough guide for the more standard events often covered by OBs. Remember in each case to avoid 'crossing the line' (use your mental TV to check that the action as seen by each camera will go in the same direction on the screen). Your aim should be to put your viewer in the best seat in the grandstand for wherever the action is – and then keep him there.

Football
Put two cameras as close to the half-way line as you can. They should be high enough to give a clear shot of the far touch-line, and far enough back to see the near touch-line

Covering football

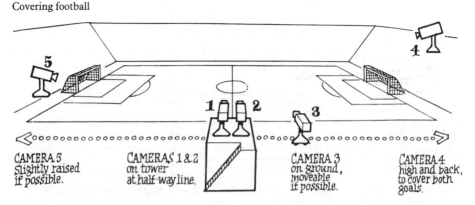

CAMERA 5
Slightly raised
if possible.

CAMERAS 1 & 2
on tower
at half-way line.

CAMERA 3
on ground,
moveable
if possible.

CAMERA 4
high and back,
to cover both
goals.

117

(if you put the cameras too near the pitch they often can't look down steeply enough to see play directly below them). Ask one cameraman to follow the play in long-shot only and the other cameraman (he should be the one with the longest zoom) to follow the play in close-up. You can cover the whole match quite adequately with this long-shot/close-up pair of cameras.

If you have a third camera, put it on the near touch-line for ground-level shots; if it can move along the touch-line, so much the better. This camera will also come in useful for interviews and the prize-giving after the match.

If you have a fourth and fifth camera, place them slightly raised behind and to the near-side of the two goals. This position is ideal for dramatic close-ups of the frantic thrashing about which often comes before a goal or an attempt at goal. If you have only four cameras, you will have to decide which is the better end – taking into account things like the position of the sun when making up your mind. Then position the fourth camera about 15–20 metres behind the near goal and 15–20 metres high. This gives the camera a clear view of both goals, and you can then record its output separately for slow-motion replays. Also remember to check that at least one of the cameras can get a good close-up of the scoreboard.

This arrangement of cameras will work for most games played on large pitches with goals at each end – games like *rugby*, *hockey*, *polo* and *American football*. Find out what colour shirts the teams will be wearing – if they are at all similar or won't contrast well in black and white, try and persuade one side to change. The home team will probably find it easier to do so.

Tennis
Games played across nets such as *tennis*, *table tennis*, *badminton* and *volleyball* tend to have smaller playing areas

Covering tennis

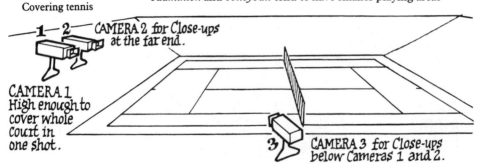

1 — 2 CAMERA 2 for Close-ups at the far end.

CAMERA 1
High enough to cover whole court in one shot.

3 CAMERA 3 for Close-ups below Cameras 1 and 2.

118

than games with goals. So the two-cameras-at-the-halfway-line technique won't work; the cameras won't be able to pan fast enough to follow the play. Instead, put the main camera at one end high enough up to be able to cover the whole playing area in one long shot. Another camera can go next to it to give close-ups of play at the far end. A third camera can be placed on the ground to cover play at the end below the other two cameras and also the players' resting positions between games. Don't forget the scoreboard. The same camera positions are also suitable for games which have small playing areas, like *snooker*.

Races

Camera positions for races on a straight course are as you might expect: a camera slightly in front of the start, a camera at the finish and a moving camera travelling alongside the course, if the course is at all long. If the course is short (not more than about two hundred metres) a camera placed behind the finish showing the contestants coming straight towards camera can be very effective.

This arrangement will cover *running*, *walking*, *swimming*, *horse*, *donkey*, *dog*, *camel*, and most other races you can think of. With *rowing* races it's effective to have a camera on a boat travelling alongside or behind the racers, if you have a camera which doesn't need to be linked to the OB unit with cables. With races round a circular track use your mental TV to check that the shots you get from each camera position maintain the continuity of direction and don't cross the line. Concentrate your coverage on the start, the final bend and the finish.

Boxing and Wrestling

Pugilistic sports like *boxing*, *wrestling*, *judo* and *karate* don't involve defending territory and so the direction you approach them from isn't as important as in other sports. One or two cameras mounted high to give long-shots and close-ups are all that's needed, but make sure they are both more or less on the same side of the ring. A camera low near the ringside can give excellent close-ups, but you have to be certain that the position is safe. Fighters often make unscheduled flying exits which can damage the cameraman and the camera as well as themselves.

Golf

To cover a complete eighteen-hole course properly you may need as many as four or five OB units. With one full-scale OB unit you will be lucky to get partial coverage of four holes – but four holes are better than nothing. Where you put your cameras depends wholly on the course lay-out.

Long Route Events

Events such as *processions*, *rallies*, *long-distance running*, *Grand Prix motor racing*, and *cycling* which take place over a long route can cause special problems. First of all you have to decide which bit of the route to concentrate on. Obviously the start, the finish, saluting bases and particularly tricky and photogenic bends are the bits which you should go for. But here once again you may find yourself severely limited by the length of cabling and the number of cameras required. A mobile tracking camera mounted on a vehicle can help with long-distance running and cycling but getting a continuous signal back to the main OB can be a difficult technical problem. Air shots from a helicopter or airship can also be very effective, but a communications engineer is essential if you are to get the full benefit of the shots from these moving cameras.

You may also find in this sort of event that it is impractical to keep all your static cameras on the same side of the route; an interesting portion of the route may run alongside a cliff, for example. The trick here is to do a 'buffer' shot with a third camera which shows the action coming towards or going away from the camera. This buffer should be used to separate the two shots which are reversing the continuity of direction.

'buffer' shots

If you haven't got a spare camera to give you a 'buffer', you can achieve almost the same effect by panning one or both of your cameras and holding a shot of the action travelling nearly straight towards or away from the camera before cutting to the next shot. Another trick which you might use is to cut to a close-up of something like a road sign or a flag and then ask the cameraman to zoom out to show what's happening on the route. The close-up then acts as a buffer shot, but obviously you can't use this trick unobtrusively more than once.

OB sound

One thing which can be tricky with OBs is getting good sound coverage. Often you may be trying to pick up sound for something which is happening at a good distance from the mike – the far corner of a polo field for example can be over 200 yards away. You will have to leave the details of the coverage to the OB engineer but it's worth swapping ideas with him; players might be persuaded to carry radio mikes, or even burying a mike in the ground might work (earth can be a good carrying medium for sound). But do make sure that you get the best possible sound of both the action and the spectators; in football, for example, the roar of the crowd often contributes as much to the excitement as the efforts of the players.

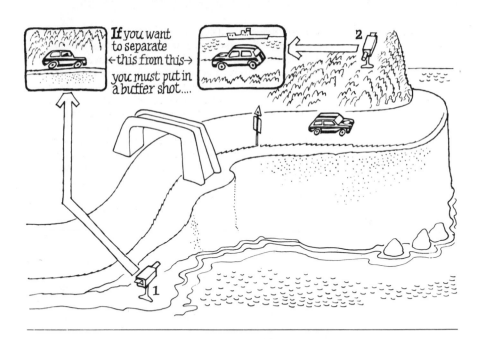

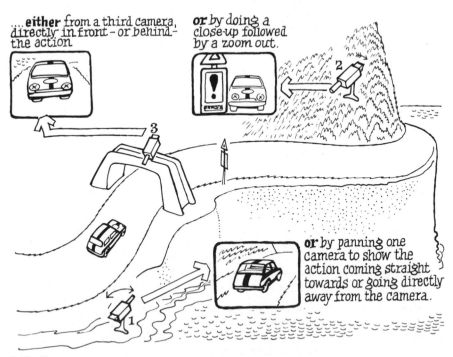

Buffer shots

the commentary box

The third major sound component (after the players and the spectators) is of course the commentator, and on your recce the OB engineer will want to know where you wish to place the commentary box. The commentator will need a mike to talk into, ear-phones to receive instructions while he is actually commentating) and a television monitor to see what the OB is transmitting. The commentary box should be positioned where he can see as much of the field of action as possible with his own eyes, so that he knows what is going on even if it isn't on camera. But he must do his commentary from the monitor, adding meaning to the shots the viewer sees and not talking about things which the viewer can't see.

But seeing is not always enough; the commentator also has to know what is going on, and keeping him supplied with information for a complicated event like an athletic meeting can be difficult. Totta's commentator, Romeo Landmark, was once left completely high and dry when the sports producer, Caesar Andante, forgot to keep him supplied with the results of the events in an army athletics meeting they were covering. So Romeo had to do his best with high jumps which he did not know the height of, long jumps which he did not know the length of and races which he did not know the times of. This was not one of Totta's most successful OBs!

SUMMARY

Outside Broadcasts

Recces are essential for OBs and the OB engineer must come with you.

The engineer will want to know

– date, time and duration of the event you want to cover

– where you want to do prize-giving ceremonies, interviews and so on

– where you want the cameras

– where you want the commentary box.

Remember to take into account where the sun will be when deciding where to put the cameras.

Make sure that none of your cameras has 'crossed the line' (the action as seen by all cameras should flow in the same direction).

Where it's impossible to avoid placing a camera on the wrong side of the action, arrange 'buffer' shots of the action coming straight towards or going straight away from the camera if you have an extra camera available.

Or pan cameras to achieve the same effect

Or use a close-up shot as a buffer and then zoom out.

OBs need a script and rehearsal just like studio programmes.

Make sure you get good sound coverage of the action and the spectators. The commentator should do his commentary from a monitor, but should also be able to see the action directly from his box. Keep him supplied with lap times, scores etc.

Publicity

You have now finished your programme, but your work isn't quite over. You still have to consider: is your programme worth publicising? The answer for all except the briefest of magazine items should be Yes.

A telephone call or note saying when the programme will be shown is always appreciated by everyone who took part. An extra paragraph in the station programme magazine together with a photograph should not be difficult to arrange. There is little to lose (and possibly a lot to gain) in contacting the local newspaper and offering them an interesting fact or two and a photograph. Or even better, write a little item about the programme yourself (they can always change it if they want to).

Of course the most powerful advertising medium of all is right in your own television station: make a short, snappy trailer. And don't forget the radio service – they are on the lookout for interesting material for their programmes like everyone else.

And finally . . .

How to make better programmes

1   Don't skip too many of the chapters in this book,
    particularly the early ones: Ideas, Research, Recce,
    Treatment.

2   Make lots of programmes. Gain experience. Learn from
    your mistakes.

3   Read books about producing programmes (if they help you).

Most Important
4   *Watch other people's films and programmes* and compare their
    approach with the way you would have tackled the same
    problems. Analyse their techniques: did they work or not?
    Use your eyes and ears intelligently while watching –
    remember nothing happens in a programme which wasn't
    made to happen by someone. Could it have been done
    better?

5   Work hard at programme-making. There are so many things
    to do and so many ways you can improve your final product
    that you can never afford to stop trying.

6   Enjoy making your programmes, and the chances are the
    viewers will enjoy watching them.

7   Be determined to make each new programme better than the
    last. Put behind you the fumbling, hit-and-miss methods
    which characterise Totta techniques. Resolve to say
    Goodbye Totter TV.

On Camera

Part Two:
BRIEFINGS

BRIEFINGS

BRIEFINGS

You should now be familiar with the procedures set out in the *Basics* part of this book and so have at your disposal a plan of action for producing and directing a programme. These *Briefings* take you one step further by looking at a selection of topics in much more detail.

Some of the material here could have been included in *Basics* but wasn't because of the risk of overloading the new producer with information; some is of interest only to those who already have a few programmes to their credit; some is designed as a handy reference only.

Use these *Briefings* in much the same way as you did *Basics*. First skim through to find out what they are about. Then go through in detail when you are ready to explore more fully the particular topic they discuss.

Briefing Number One
The Right Words

The right words are important when you are talking to other television people. A camera for example can move in twelve different ways; it can also move in as many as four at the same time (though this would be unusual). It's important therefore that the cameraman is given something more specific than 'Can you – er – point it over there?'

Let's start with the shot sizes. (See illustration p. 128)

1   *The Right Words to Describe Shots*
The usual names and abbreviations for shots are:

Long Shot (LS	Medium Close-up (MCU)
Medium Long Shot (MLS)	Close-up (CU)
Mid-shot (MS)	Big Close-up (BCU)

There is also a Very Long Shot (VLS) which, as the name implies, is even further out than the Long Shot.

These shot sizes vary slightly from place to place and over periods of time. For example, it's probably true that all present-day shot sizes are closer in than they used to be. But

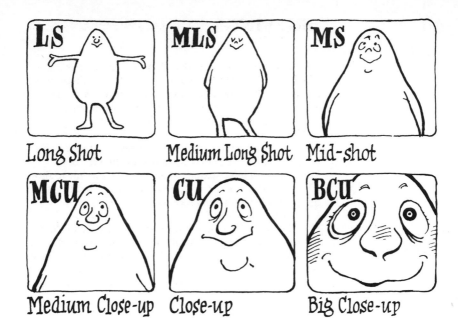

LS — Long Shot

MLS — Medium Long Shot

MS — Mid-shot

MCU — Medium Close-up

CU — Close-up

BCU — Big Close-up

the descriptions above are sufficiently accurate to give everyone a common starting point for taking shots of people – they don't make much sense applied to cars and buildings, for example.

The *Long Shot* covers the whole height of a person and also gives viewers a chance to see something of the background. The *Medium Long Shot* cuts the body at about knee level; it's by nature unsatisfying since it's not wide enough to show much of the background nor close enough to show much detail of the person. The *Mid-shot* cuts just below the elbows and is fine for introductory shots for interviews; if held for too long, however, the viewer soon tires of looking at the clothes which occupy most of the screen. The face is the main point of interest in an interview – far better to cut to the *Medium Close-up* and save the viewer straining his eyes to see more of the face on the screen. The Medium Close-up cuts just below the armpits and is just close enough to show detail on a person's face without being so close that it intrudes. This is the standard comfortable shot for interviews in the small screen world of television. With the *Close-up* (cutting at the collar) the shot has become intimate. Or it seems to be putting the subject under pressure, if the interview is a confrontation rather than a chat. With the *Big Close-up* the feelings of intimacy and confrontation come over even more forcefully, strong feelings for a director to bring into play. But if used too often the Big Close-up loses its impact and becomes tiresome.

2   *The Right Words for the Cameraman*
Camera movements can be divided into two – those which involve moving the camera over the ground and those which don't.

There are several points to note about these instructions to cameramen.

a   The instructions are correct for both studio and cameras on location. In practice, however, instructions to **location** cameramen are far less formal than those to studio cameramen. The reason for this is that your relationship with the location cameraman is very different: you talk to him face-to-face instead of at a distance over the talkback; you can't talk to him while he is shooting (it would ruin the sound); there's only one of him. But you should use the right words for directing on location just as you should in the studio.

'camera right'   b   Whenever you are near a camera, use 'right' and 'left' to
and 'camera left'   refer to the camera's view of the scene. So always describe directions as if you were standing where the camera is positioned (even if you are standing in front of the camera and facing it, when your right and left are the reverse of the camera's). In fact to show that they are looking at things from the camera's point of view and not their own, people in television usually use the terms 'camera right' and 'camera left', and so should you.

c   You may have noticed that the right words all end with '*to* . . .' (except for '*elevate*' and '*depress*'). This is to remind you that it is important to tell the cameraman to what you want him to move ('*pan right to the photograph*', '*move left slightly to bring the interviewee's head away from the flowers*', '*zoom in to a close-up of the statue*'). Unless you give the reason for the move by specifying to what he should move, the cameraman has to guess at your intentions, and this is not a good way for you to direct. Of course you need only specify where you want the camera to move to during the rehearsal: during the recording or transmission a reminder ('*pan right*' or '*zoom in*') is all that is needed. If you want a camera move to stop, say '. . . *and steady*' or '*steady it there*'.

3   *The Right Words for Sound*
You need worry about instructions to the sound man only when he is playing something back into the programme; he

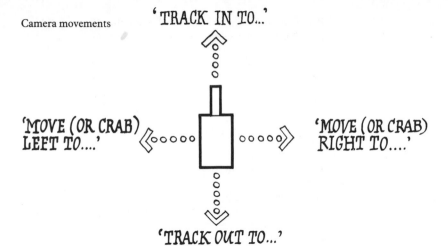

'TRACK IN TO...'

'MOVE (OR CRAB) LEFT TO....'

'MOVE (OR CRAB) RIGHT TO....'

'TRACK OUT TO...'

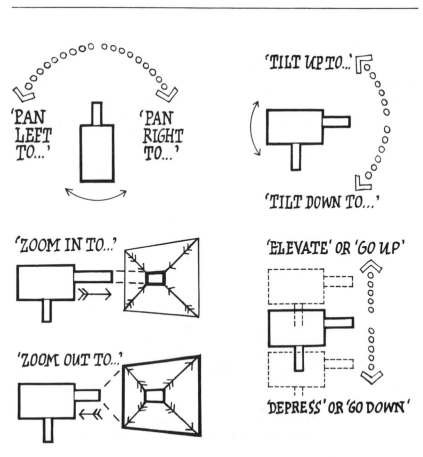

'PAN LEFT TO...'

'PAN RIGHT TO...'

'TILT UP TO...'

'TILT DOWN TO...'

'ZOOM IN TO...'

'ZOOM OUT TO...'

'ELEVATE' OR 'GO UP'

'DEPRESS' OR 'GO DOWN'

takes his own cue for recording. The normal expression is *'go grams'* or *'go tape'* but *'fade up sound'* is also acceptable (don't forget to tell him during the rehearsal at what speed you want him to fade up the sound, *'slowly'*, *'quickly'*, *'very gently'* and so on). At the beginning of a programme it always looks better if the sound comes up slightly before the picture. So start the sound first *('go tape')*; then when you hear the sound bring up the picture *('fade up 2')*. If you want the sound man to stop whatever he is playing back, say *'fade down sound'* or *'stop sound'* or *'lose sound'*. At the end of the programme say *'fade sound and vision'*; once again it looks good if the sound goes first and the picture fades a fraction later.

4   *The Right Words for Telecine (TK) and Videotape (VT)*
To start, just say *'run TK'* or *'run VT'*. If you have more than one machine allocated to your programme, you can mention the number of the machine *('run TK3')*, but in practice the operator will know from the rehearsal which machine you want. You should also have mentioned the number of the machine when you (or your assistant) asked the operator to standby: *'standby TK3'*. The operator replies to this and any other request you make by pressing his buzzer once for *'yes'*, twice for *'no'*; obviously with this system he can't answer more than one question at a time. Acknowledge any message on the buzzer with *'Thank you, VT'* (or TK). You don't usually have to bother to stop TK or VT (they take their own cue) but if you do, just say *'stop TK'* or *'stop VT'*.

If you want the operator to go back to the beginning of his insert(s), say *'Reset VT'* (or TK), specifying the insert if there is more than one. If you don't need TK or VT for part of the rehearsal, tell them so that they can relax – it's a strain trying to stay alert over a long period when nothing happens.

5   *The Right Words for Lights*
'Up lights', *'down lights'*, *'dim lights'*, or just *'lights'* (the lighting man should know what to do from the script and the rehearsal).

6   *The Right Words for the Floor Manager*
During recording or transmission most of your instructions to the floor manager (usually known as the FM) are to do with cueing contributors to the programme. The instructions for this are quite straightforward: *'cue Jack'* or *'cue Jill'*. But because human beings (both the floor manager and the contributor) take time to react, and because it's Totter television to have someone on screen waiting for his cue, make sure that the cue is given before you cut to the

cue and cut

picture. So always say '*cue and cut*' in that order. Have no fear that the contributor will start before the vision mixer has cut to the picture – punching up a shot takes no time at all, starting up takes a good half second.

At the end of an interview in the studio it's usual to say '*one minute to go*', '*30 seconds to go*' and with 15 seconds to go '*wind him (or her) up*'. The floor manager signals this to the interviewer. Keep the interviewer's shot off the screen while the floor manager is signalling to him.

If you want the floor manager to stop the rehearsal or recording, say '*Hold it*'. To avoid confusion, don't use this term to halt a camera movement.

7 *The Right Words to the Vision Mixer*
By the end of the rehearsal the vision mixer should know as much about the picture cues as the director. So your instructions during the transmission and recording are merely an indication of when to do something. A trained vision mixer can react very quickly to a correct command, but it's helpful to give him some warning of when the instruction is coming. So get into the habit of saying which camera or what you want next ('*two next*' or '*VT next*' or '*TK next*') followed by '*and . . . two*', or '*and . . . VT*', or '*and . . . TK*'. The '*and*' should be a bit drawn out; the '*two*', '*VT*' or '*TK*' should be said crisply, as that marks the point at which you wish to cut. This system also works with mixes, wipes, supers and so on. Simply say '*mix to two next . . .*(pause) *. . . and mix*'.

Some directors like to say '*coming to two*' instead of '*two next*'. Fine – it doesn't matter which you say as long as you get into the habit of giving a warning.

checking ahead

The warning is helpful not only for the cameramen and vision mixers but also benefits you the director, because saying '*two next*' reminds you to look at the monitor to check that camera two's shot is as you want it. You should get into the habit of checking ahead, even when your assistant is saying '*two next*' for you, as he or she would do in a drama or any tightly scripted programme. The monitor-checking habit will save you from many embarrassing mistakes, for example, cutting to a camera with the same size shot of what you already have on the screen, or cutting to a shot before it is in focus.

8 *The Right Words for Everyone*
Some general points which apply to all studio direction:

132

who – what – when

a There are at least a dozen people listening to you giving instructions over the talk-back and so you must always announce whom you are talking to first. *'Camera three – zoom in to close-up'*, *'Sound – can we have the effects louder, please?'*
Who – what – when is the order to follow when directing.

standby

b *'Standby'* is a word to alert people: *'standby TK'*, *'standby studio'*.
But don't overuse it. Imagine the irritation of someone who has heard your first *'standby'*, is standing by and then has to listen to you saying *'standby'* several more times. If it's TK or VT, they will have given you a buzz after your first *'standby'*; if it's a cameraman you are asking to standby, he will be offering you the shot on his monitor or will nod his camera up and down in acknowledgement (waving it from side to side means *'no'*). So further standbys are not necessary – they merely raise people's blood pressure, not their alertness. One *'standby'* is enough!

c When you are directing you don't want to waste time looking for the next shot in the script. So write over the typewritten camera numbers and other instructions with a pencil, using large letters which can be instantly seen. Like this:

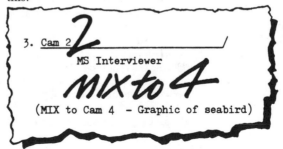

3. Cam 2
MS Interviewer
MIX to 4
(MIX to Cam 4 - Graphic of seabird)

d If you interrupt a rehearsal for refreshment announce clearly the length of the break and the time for restarting. *'Ten minutes break, everyone. Restart at quarter past eleven'*.

e Studio recordings usually start with putting on the clock – this identifies the tape and (like a film leader) gives the videotape operator something on which to set up the tape for playback. The VT clock (which is specially designed for television) is put in front of a convenient camera and when the videotape machines are running the director says *'Start the clock'*. The floor manager starts the clock. With 10 seconds to go the floor manager starts counting aloud *'10,9,8,7,6,5,4,3'*. At 3 the secretary in the gallery takes over the counting and the vision mixer fades to black. With

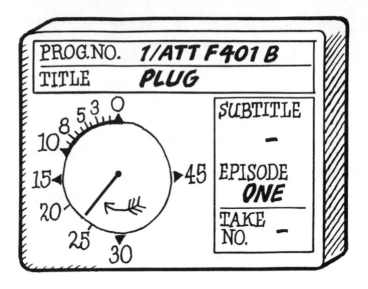

VT clock

one second to go the director says '*Go tape*' or '*Run VT*' and
'*Fade up . . . and cue*'. If you are recording an interview it's
usual to cut to a shot of the interviewee instead of fading to
black at 3; this gives you a bit of extra shot for safety which
can also be used to introduce the interviewee from the
studio.

f   Don't forget to say '*Please*' and '*Thank you*' occasionally
during the rehearsal. No one expects you to do so during the
recording or transmission. But everyone likes to know that
you do have these words in your vocabulary (and the
thought in your mind). At the end of your programme say
'*Thank you, everybody*' over the talkback.

g   After a recording wait for the technical manager to sample
the recording and pronounce it OK before letting anyone
leave the studio.

SUMMARY BRIEFING NUMBER ONE

The Right Words

for *shots:*

— very long shot

— long shot

— medium long shot

— mid-shot

— medium close-up

— close-up

— big close-up.

for the *cameraman:*

— track in/out to . . .

— move (crab) right/left to . . .

— pan right/left to . . .

— tilt up/down to . . .

— zoom in/out to . . .

— elevate (go up)

— depress (go down)

— camera right/left (to identify sides)

— . . . and steady.

for *sound:*

— go grams/tape *or* fade up sound

— fade down sound *or* stop sound *or* lose sound

— fade sound and vision (at the end of the
  programme).

Always start sound before vision at the beginning of the
programme.

for *telecine* and *videotape:*

— run TK/VT

— stop TK/VT

— standby TK/VT (one buzz means yes; two buzzes, no)

for *lights:*

— lights

— up lights

— down lights or dim lights.

for the *floor manager* (FM):

— cue Jack

— one minute to go, 30 seconds to go, etc.

— wind him (or her) up

— hold it.

Always cue before cutting – say 'Cue and cut'.

for the *vision mixer:*

— two next . . . and . . . two *or* coming to two . . . and . . .

— two

— mix to two next . . . and . . . mix.

When you say 'Two next' check the shot on two

General Points

When directing in the studio always follow the order who – what – when.

One 'standby' is enough.

Cameramen nod camera up and down for 'yes', sideways for 'no'.

Write out direction notes on the script BIG.

Don't forget the clock at the beginning of studio recordings.

The occasional 'please' and 'thank you' is welcome.

Say 'Thank you, everybody' at the end of the programme.

At the end of a recording wait for the technical manager to check the recording before letting the studio go.

Briefing Number Two
If Technology Turns You Off, Read On . . .

Some brains seize up at the thought of anything technical. Television and video technology is complicated – so the attitude is understandable. But the basic ideas which make television possible are straightforward enough to be grasped by even the most untechnical of people. It's certainly worth the effort. At best you will begin to appreciate some of the beautiful ingenuities of video. At the very least you will realise that not everything the engineers say and do has to be a closed book.

A First Look at the System
Television is light. For colour television you need just three colours of light: red, green and blue. These are known as the primary colours; by mixing them together in different proportions you can produce for television any colour you wish. The three colours added together make white light; black is the absence of light.

The electronic camera has inside it three tubes, one for each primary colour. Light entering the camera is split into the three primary colours and each of the tubes continuously measures the amount of its primary colour in the picture by scanning it with an electron beam in the same way your eyes are scanning this book: left to right, line by line, working from top to bottom. In North America, Japan and a few other places each television page (or picture) has 525 lines; in most other places it has 625 lines. The information about the colours from the three tubes is turned into a signal (in a process known as 'encoding') which can be conveyed to the viewer's television receiver by cable, videotape or broadcasting (using a transmitter and aerial). There are three different systems of encoding in general use today, PAL, NTSC and SECAM. These stand for Phase Alternate Line, National Television Systems Committee and (the French for) Sequential Colour with Memory (SECAM was devised in France).

The television set which the viewer watches does the same thing as the camera, but in reverse. It receives the encoded signal from the transmitter and breaks it down into three separate signals, one for each of the primary colours. The screen of the television set has many thousands of groups of three phosphor dots (called 'triads'), again one dot for each primary colour.

These dots glow when they are struck by the beams coming from the electron guns in the television set, with each dot reproducing exactly the same amount of its primary colour as the camera found at that point in the original picture. Because the dots are so small and so close together, the viewer's eyes blur them all into one picture, a picture which is of course almost identical to the one in front of the camera.

This operation of analysing and recreating the picture – known as scanning – takes place at an incredible speed: 30 times a second in North America, 25 times a second elsewhere, far too fast for you to see. It's very important that the electron beams in the camera are exactly in step with each other so that the three pictures from the three tubes will lie precisely on top of each other when they are reproduced in the receiver – in other words, that the camera is 'registering' correctly. It's this process, and the colour balance, which the engineers have to check during the 'line-up' period which precedes the recording or transmission of programmes in the studio.

Modern single tube colour cameras sidestep the registration problem by analysing the scene as a single picture. The electron beam scans the light from the scene after it has passed through a mask which splits it into very fine slivers of red, green and blue and this signal is then encoded in the normal way. Making one tube do the job of three results in some loss of definition (the signal has less information to define the picture) but single tube cameras are on the verge of being adopted as standard for professional newsgathering.

Encoding the Video Signal – 4 into 1 Must Go
Let's start again with the camera.
Think of the camera as a piece of equipment for converting light variations into electrical variations or signals. The colour camera then has four jobs to do: it has to produce a signal for red, a signal for green and a signal for blue. It also has to produce a signal for black and white television sets – why should black and white viewers miss the programme? In theory there is no reason why each of these four signals shouldn't be conveyed to the receiving sets separately – in other words you could have four transmitters, four cables or four videotape machines each feeding a signal to the receiving set. Plus an extra transmitter, cable or tape machine for the sound, of course.

It's easy to see that such a system would be impossibly cumbersome and expensive. Quite besides the fact that, as far as broadcasting is concerned, the airwaves are crowded enough as it is: finding the room to transmit five different signals for every TV channel would be impossible.

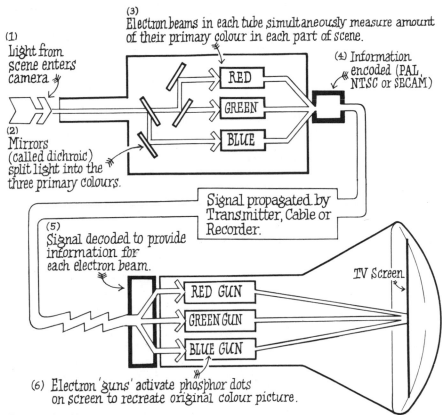

(1) Light from scene enters camera

(3) Electron beams in each tube, simultaneously measure amount of their primary colour in each part of scene.

(4) Information encoded (PAL, NTSC or SECAM)

RED

GREEN

BLUE

(2) Mirrors (called dichroic) split light into the three primary colours.

Signal propagated by Transmitter, Cable or Recorder.

(5) Signal decoded to provide information for each electron beam.

RED GUN

GREEN GUN

BLUE GUN

TV Screen

(6) Electron 'guns' activate phosphor dots on screen to recreate original colour picture.

Transmitting colour

So how can you cut down on this duplication? One way of reducing it makes use of a peculiarity in the way we see things: the human eye can't focus on colour as well as it can on black and white. Think how blurred a colour comic would look if all the hard black outlines were removed. This is also the reason we see continuous colour on the TV screen, not the thousands of tiny blobs of colour it really consists of.

So the camera converts the picture into two sets of electrical signals: a black and white signal known as *luminance* to convey all the detail, and a *chrominance* signal which carries the colour information. Because of our blind spot for colour detail the chrominance signal need only be low definition (which also has advantages when it comes to combining it with the luminance signal). In fact television works like a careless comic book artist; first it draws a detailed black and white picture and then it roughly fills in the colours. If you freeze an uncluttered picture on the screen and look carefully at something with a hard outline (like a person's nose in profile) you can see this slapdash approach to colour at work – the colour often visibly overlaps the outline.

So four signals have now been reduced to two: luminance and chrominance. But how do you get a black and white signal (the luminance signal) out of a camera with three colour tubes? The answer is: go back to first principles.

the luminance signal

Red, green and blue light, as we have seen, produce white light; the exact mix is 30% red, 59% green and 11% blue. The camera adds up the output from its three colour tubes in these proportions to produce the luminance signal. The strength of the signal varies with the brightness of the picture. A very bright area of picture will produce a strong luminance signal (white); a dark area of the picture will produce a weak luminance signal (dark grey or black). So by adding together the output of the three colour tubes in the correct proportions the camera produces a signal which defines all the shades of grey between white and black. This is the signal we see on black and white sets. It's also the signal which defines the detail for colour viewers.

the chrominance signal

How does the camera arrive at the chrominance signal? Not – as you might expect – by encoding the output of each of the three colour tubes separately. This after all would duplicate information which is already in the luminance signal (red + green + blue = white). Instead the camera produces signals for just two colours, red and blue, chosen because they account for only 30% and 11% of white light and are therefore easier to include in the complete signal. The proportion for the third colour, green, can be worked out in the receiver by subtracting the values for red and blue from the luminance signal – in effect any brightness in the picture which isn't accounted for by the red and blue signals must come from the green. To make the signals easier to transmit red and blue are encoded as the values remaining after the luminance signal has been subtracted from the output of each colour tube. In other words they are encoded as two *colour difference* signals which together make up the chrominance signal. It sounds complicated when written out in full but if you look at it as a set of equations it's easier to understand.

We are still at the point where the camera has reduced the four signals needed for colour television to two: luminance and chrominance. The next stage in the compression process – getting all this information into one video signal – involves technical ingenuities which are difficult to appreciate

ENCODING COLOUR AS EQUATIONS

R = red   G = green   B = blue   Y = luminance (or brightness)

The camera adds the output from the colour tubes to produce the luminance signal. $R + G + B = Y$.

It also produces $R - Y$ and $B - Y$.

The receiver uses Y without further processing.

It decodes R–Y and B–Y by adding Y

$(R - Y) + Y = R$

$(B - Y) + Y = B$

$Y - R - B = G$

without an understanding of the basic principles of radio. Briefly, however, the colour difference signals can be confined to a small section of the spectrum because the chrominance signal, as we have seen, only needs to be low definition (written in shorthand, as it were, instead of the longhand needed for the luminance signal). By packaging this colour information with a carrier* whose frequency is chosen because it can be slotted into the least used part of the spectrum occupied by the luminance signal, both chrominance and luminance can be sent as one signal. It's rather like squeezing a shorthand message into the blank bits on the address half of a picture postcard.

Of course all this information about brightness and colour won't reproduce a picture at all if the various parts of the camera and receiver aren't working exactly in sync with each other. So the TV signal, besides brightness and colour

*A carrier is a device for converting information into a more manageable form. In electrical terms a carrier starts off as a regular electrical wave which is then modulated (or changed) in frequency, amplitude or phase by the signal it is combined with. This signal is transmitted to the receiver which recovers the original signal by separating it from the carrier. Without the carrier it would be impossible to transmit the signal at all; it would also be impossible to give viewers a choice of channel. It's rather like distributing sausages – first you put the mixture into skins, with different-sized skins for different types of sausage. Then you send the sausages off on strings. The receiver recognises the sausage type by the skin (even if it has been squashed in transit). And of course the contents of the sausage aren't affected by the carrier.

The signal for one line of television picture

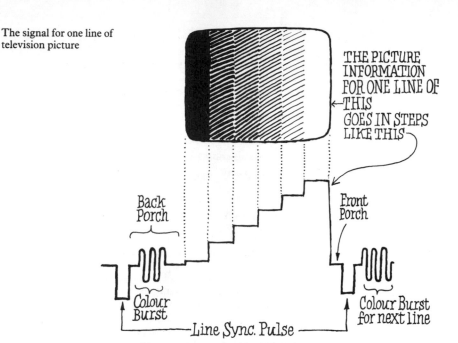

THE PICTURE INFORMATION FOR ONE LINE OF ←THIS GOES IN STEPS LIKE THIS→

Back Porch

Front Porch

Colour Burst

Colour Burst for next line

—Line Sync. Pulse—

information, contains a whole range of purely technical information: line sync pulses to cue the electron beams to fly back to begin a new line (at the rate of 15,625 pulses per second!), a colour burst signal to enable the colour information to be decoded correctly, and so on. The complete colour TV signal is a complicated affair.

This is a very simplified version of how colour is encoded in the NTSC and PAL systems, but it does give you an idea of their beautiful ingenuity. The PAL system is a refinement of NTSC and gives better colour fidelity by comparing the signals from successive lines and displaying an average for the two lines. NTSC can't do this and so is prone to colour distortions. This is why NTSC sets have a knob to adjust the hue and many engineers irreverently refer to NTSC as Never Twice the Same Colour (PAL is blessed with Pictures Always Lovely and SECAM with System Essentially Contrary to the American Method). SECAM, though a French invention, is the standard for Russia and Eastern Europe and works on a different system. It transmits each colour difference signal on alternate lines. None of the systems are compatible so unless you have special playback equipment programmes from other systems will usually have to be converted.

Two Fields Make a Frame
Moving pictures are an illusion; video and film pictures are

in fact static. They only appear to move because of a phenomenon known as persistence of vision. Our eyes continue to see a picture for a fraction of a second after it has disappeared; if a second picture appears while the memory of the first persists the eye merges the two pictures together. So the movement we see on the screen is the result of a rapid succession of stills.

The scanning rate of 25 frames a second (30 for 525 lines) is more than enough to fool the eye into believing that it is seeing movement on the screen. But this speed isn't enough to stop the eye seeing a flicker between each frame. Film gets over the problem by showing each frame twice. Television gets over the problem by a process known as *interlacing*; the picture is scanned not line by line but on alternate lines, first all the odd lines, then all the even lines. Each alternate line scan is known as a field and is scanned in one fiftieth (or sixtieth) of a second. Each field of 625 line television has $312\frac{1}{2}$ lines; two fields make one frame.* The eye blends the fields together just as it blends successive frames into each other. So movement appears smooth on the screen and the flicker once every fiftieth of a second is too fast for the eye to see. (See illustration on next page).

Teletext In fact not all the $312\frac{1}{2}$ lines in a field are used for picture information. The scanning beam needs time to fly back to the top of the screen; it also needs time to settle down when it gets there. So the beam doesn't actually carry any picture information till about line 23 of the first field and line 336 of the second. These 'spare' lines at the top of the picture can be used to transmit the coded information known as teletext – you can see the signal as a narrow twinkling black and white band at the top of the screen if you adjust the vertical hold to let the picture slip. To use teletext your receiver needs a decoder to unscramble what is being transmitted; you need a keypad to select the 'page' you want from the index.

Video Recording

It's difficult now to think of television without videotape, but for the first two decades of television (1936 onwards) there was no satisfactory way of recording electronic pictures. Pointing a film camera at a picture tube was the technique most often used; this technique, however, produced telerecordings which were both expensive and poor quality.

The idea that you can record an electrical signal by magnetising a tape and then replay it without further processing had already been developed into a practical device for audio before the Second World War. It seemed an

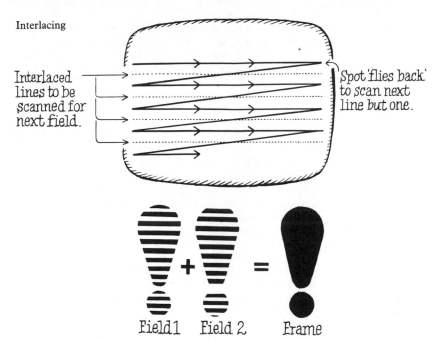

Interlaced lines to be scanned for next field.

Spot 'flies back' to scan next line but one.

Field 1   Field 2   Frame

obvious next step to adapt this audio technology to record the continuous electrical signal produced by the camera but the far greater range and quantity of information in the video signal made it a difficult problem to crack.

Magnetic tape is a continuous strip of bar magnets whose north and south poles can be realigned by drawing them past a tiny gap in the head of an electromagnet. This turns the magnetic field round the tape into a copy of the magnetic field round the head. This copy can then be 'read' by reversing the process: in other words, using the field round the tape to alter the field round the head. This is what happens when you play back a tape.

Colur television needs a spread of about 18 octaves* to accommodate its signal; audio needs about 10 (for the technically minded, 50 Hz to 5·5 MHz for TV, 20 to 20,000 Hz for audio). By manipulating the video signal and combining it with a frequency modulated carrier (FM) the range of the signal can be reduced to about 5 octaves – the spectrum chosen for this is usually from 500 kHz to 16 MHz. But these are very high frequencies for magnetic tape to cope with. At the upper end of this frequency range information is arriving so fast (at 16 million bits per second) that it swamps the recording capacity of the tape, which is limited by the size of the gap in the recording head, the size

*An octave is the range between any frequency and double the same frequency. So 20–40 Hz is one octave; 40–80 Hz is another

of the bar magnets on the tape and the speed at which the magnets are passing the head. Since it's obviously impractical to go on reducing the width of the head gap and the fineness of the magnetic powder on the tape indefinitely, the only way magnetic tape can be adapted to handle the video signal is to increase the speed of the tape past the head (the writing speed). The arithmetic suggests that a speed of about 15 metres per second is needed; this means that one hour's recording would use up 55 kilometres of tape (about a third more than the width of the English Channel). Clearly impractical.

2 inch format

*Ampex's memorable name has nothing to do with amps but comes from the initials of the company's founder, Alexander M. Poniatoff, and the first syllable of the word 'excellent'.

2 inch Quadruplex format

The answer to the problem is to have more than one head and to move the head as well as the tape. The first practical videotape (brought out by Ampex* in 1955) used four heads mounted on a drum spinning at 240 revolutions per second for 525 lines (250 revs for 625 lines). The 50 mm (2 inch) wide tape was drawn past the head drum at a speed of just under 38.1 centimetres (15 inches) per second. This arrangement produced an effective writing speed of 137 kilometres per hour (about 90 mph).

The tracks on 2 inch tape are laid almost at right angles with the edge of the tape. Only one of the four heads is in contact with the tape at a time so that each head lays down about 16 lines of a 312½ line field with each pass. This makes it impossible to show a still frame on the screen if the tape isn't

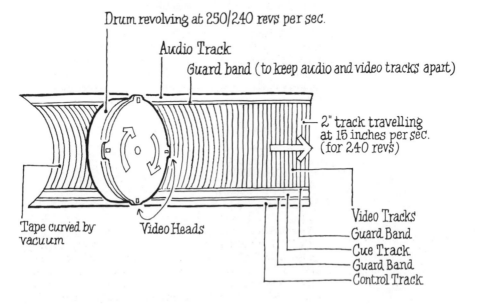

Drum revolving at 250/240 revs per sec.

Audio Track

Guard band (to keep audio and video tracks apart)

2" track travelling at 15 inches per sec. (for 240 revs)

Tape curved by vacuum

Video Heads

Video Tracks
Guard Band
Cue Track
Guard Band
Control Track

moving – the heads would simply be repeating the same 16 lines over and over again, enough to produce only a narrow strip of picture on the screen. But this 2 inch quadruplex or 'transverse scan' format (quad for short) produces excellent pictures and has successfully served as the standard format for professional broadcasting for 25 years. The cost, size and weight of machine and tapes, however, have made it unsuitable for wider use.

Helical Scan

Helical scan is the system which has taken over from quad. In doing so it has revolutionised video and is now virtually standard for both professional and domestic machines.

There are many types of helical scan on the market, most of them unfortunately incompatible with each other. Broadly speaking, however, modern helical scan can be split into two categories by the way the tape is wrapped round the head drum: open Omega and closed Omega.

Open Omega

The open Omega wrap is used for all cassette machines as it is easier to lace up automatically. Two heads are mounted opposite each other in the drum so that one head is always in contact with the tape. The speeds of the drum and the tape are so arranged that each head records one field diagonally across the tape each time it passes.

Closed Omega

With the closed Omega wrap there is only one head for recording and replay but because the gap in the tape path round the drum is very small, the loss of signal at this point can be disguised. For this type of machine the drum has to revolve at 3000 revolutions per minute, which is twice the speed needed for the open Omega wrap. The closed Omega generally gives better pictures but because it costs more to build a head drum which can operate at such speed it is used only for professional open-reel video machines.

Open Omega wrap   Closed Omega wrap

EACH HEAD RECORDS ONE FIELD DIAGONALLY ACROSS TAPE

SINGLE HEAD RECORDS ONE FIELD PER REVOLUTION

— Each line = one field —

(Omega wraps are named after the Greek Letter Ω)

With both types of helical scan the tape leaves the drum one tape width higher than the point at which it first came into contact, either because the drum is mounted at a slight angle (open Omega) or because the feed and take-up spools are mounted at different heights (closed Omega). In both systems the tape path round the drum is shaped like part of a spiral – or in mathematical language, like part of a helix. Hence the name, helical scan.

Helical scan has made it possible to simplify the electronics in the recorder as well as reduce the width of the tape. Because the tracks are laid diagonally along the tape they can be made much longer than with transverse scan and each track in fact represents one complete field. This makes it possible to produce a still frame on the screen even when the tape isn't moving (the drum merely scans the same field over and over again and each field is shown twice to give the semblance of a complete frame). It also makes it possible to show the picture at double speed (the machine scans every other track) or at half speed (the machine scans every track twice). True fast and slow motion isn't possible with normal video because you can't adjust the scanning speed in the camera; with film you can of course adjust the 'scan' by exposing fewer or more frames per second.

The pace of progress in the design of video heads, tapes and circuitry seems to be speeding up rather than slackening off and it's no exaggeration (even if it's a cliché) to say that we are at the beginning of a revolution in the use of the medium. Every few months cheaper, lighter and better quality cameras and recorders are brought on to the market. At present the trend is to combine both camera and recorder in one package using a $\frac{1}{2}$ inch format (which unfortunately once again is not compatible with existing $\frac{1}{2}$ inch formats). A $\frac{1}{4}$ inch camera/recorder combination is also round the corner. In fact it's safe to say that with digital video recording waiting in the wings and the increasing use of computer technology in video it's only a matter of time before magnetic videotape shrinks so much that it disappears altogether and is replaced by the solid-state memories used for computers. When that happens video will be as accessible as the pocket calculator.

A GUIDE TO VIDEO FORMATS

2 inch (50 mm) or quadruplex (quad)	professional standard, no longer manufactured. Being replaced by 1 inch.
1 inch (25 mm)	the new professional standard. Open reel tapes, not cassette. Available in 3 types: A, B and C, all incompatible. B is widely used in Europe, particularly Spain and West Germany. C is the most widely used in Britain.
$\frac{3}{4}$ inch (19 mm) U-matic	two versions: high-band and low-band. High-band is considered broadcast quality for news and topical programmes. Low-band is cheaper. High-band cassettes played on low-band machines give an unstable picture; low-band cassettes can be played on high-band machines, but only in black and white.
$\frac{1}{2}$ inch (12.5 mm)	two systems: Sony's Betamax, and VHS (Video Home System). The most popular formats for domestic use.
Video 2000	The European answer to Betamax and VHS. Uses only half the width of the tape for a recording so that the tape is reversible.
$\frac{1}{4}$ inch (6 mm)	same size as audio cassette tape. Is this the format of the future?

SUMMARY BRIEFING NUMBER TWO

If Technology Turns You Off, Read On . . .

A first look . . .

All television colours can be made by combining in varying proportions the three primary colours – red, green and blue.

The three colours added together in the correct proportions make white light. Black is the absence of all light.

Three tubes inside the camera analyse the proportion of each primary colour at each point by scanning the picture in unison. This information is encoded (by PAL, NTSC or SECAM) and transmitted to the viewer's set, which then reverses the procedure to produce a picture.

Groups of three dots on the screen (which correspond with the measuring points in the original picture) reproduce exactly the same amount of each primary colour as in the original. The viewer's eye merges the three dots into one. With each picture being scanned 25 times a second the original picture is created on the screen.

Engineers use line-up mainly to check that the scanning beams in the tubes are working in unison, and that the red, green and blue outputs from the camera are correctly balanced.

Encoding the signal

The camera produces a *luminance* signal by adding up the output of the three colour tubes. It also produces two *colour difference* signals which make up the *chrominance* signal. Luminance, chrominance and synchronising pulses are combined to form the complete video signal.

Two fields make a frame

25 frames a second is fast enough to make pictures appear to move, but not fast enough to eliminate flicker. Hence 'interlacing' – scanning alternate lines.

Two $312\frac{1}{2}$ line fields make one 625 line frame.

Teletext uses 'spare' lines at the top of each field.

Video Recording

To record the video signal on magnetic tape a high 'writing' speed (head to tape speed) is necessary. This is achieved by mounting the video head(s) on a fast spinning drum.

The quad system uses four video heads and lays tracks across 2 inch tape. Freeze frames aren't normally possible on quad machines.

With helical scan each track laid diagonally along the tape contains one field, making possible freeze frames and (a sort of) fast and slow motion. There are two main types of helical scan wrap: open Omega and closed Omega.

Magnetic videotape will disappear; the future lies with computer-type memories.

Briefing Number Three
Chromakey

Question: how do you put a person into a photograph?

Answer: photograph the person, cut him out of the print and stick this cut-out on the picture.

That basically is what you are doing when you use chromakey, also known as colour separation overlay, or CSO. Except with CSO it works like this: you put the photograph in front of one camera in the studio and you put the person in front of another. Instead of scissors to cut the person out of the background, you colour the background blue and adjust the camera to leave everything that's blue out of the picture. This electronic cut-out is then superimposed on the photograph. And there you are – you have put the person into the photograph and you have done it by using CSO.

Let's look at some of the points in more detail.

The Photograph
This can be a painting, drawing, diagram or a complete set in the studio. The picture can even come from the caption scanner or TK or VT – in fact anything you want to provide a background. If you want your CSO to be effective and realistic, the picture should have some depth in it and should also be very slightly out of focus (as the background of pictures usually are if you look carefully).

The Person
This of course can be as many people – or things – as you like. The only limitation is that nothing which you want to see in your final CSO shot must be blue or wearing blue, because the camera on this set (called the foreground set) will exclude everything blue, without exception. So watch out for blue shirts, ties, jewellery and so on.

It can be difficult to get the lighting on the person to match the lighting in the picture and so you will have to allow time for this to be done properly. If you want to create the illusion of the person being inside the picture really effectively, it's a good idea to have some props in the foreground set which match props in the picture – similar chairs, a vase of flowers, a bush or tree for outdoor scenes. Used carefully these props can give a sense of depth to the whole scene.

TO GET INTO THIS

DO THIS »»

FOREGROUND | BACKGROUND

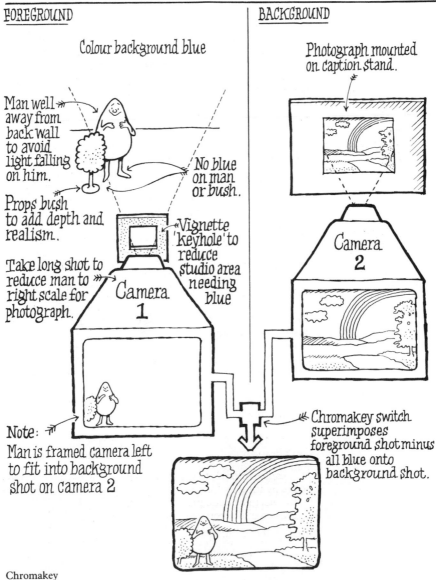

Colour background blue

Man well away from back wall to avoid light falling on him.

Props bush to add depth and realism.

Take long shot to reduce man to right scale for photograph.

No blue on man or bush.

'Vignette 'keyhole' to reduce studio area needing blue

Camera 1

Photograph mounted on caption stand.

Camera 2

Chromakey switch superimposes foreground shot minus all blue onto background shot.

Note:
Man is framed camera left to fit into background shot on camera 2

Chromakey

Blue

Blue is the colour most commonly used for the disappearing bits in CSO because it's the colour there is the least of in human skin. But you can in fact use any other colour for the things you want to leave out, and sometimes there may be a good reason for doing so, especially if there are no people involved in your CSO shot.

Let's stay with the blue. The colour can come from using a blue curtain as a backing, blue paint or blue light on the cyclorama. If you are using blue light, make sure the person keeps well out of it as any blue light which spills onto him will cause an unpleasant fuzzy effect round his outline, especially round his hair. This can sometimes be difficult to get rid of.

the vignette

If you want the person in your foreground shot to appear very small in relation to the background picture, it may be necessary to take a very long shot of him, a shot that takes in much more of the studio than it is practical to cover with blue. In such cases it is possible to put a blue frame (called a 'vignette') in front of the camera to limit the area of the studio which the camera can see. Only this much reduced studio area need then be given a blue background. It's rather like making the camera look through a keyhole instead of an open door. The vignette, by the way, will have to be lit, which could take a little time.

Getting the size of the person right in relation to the photograph can be tricky. Once you have got it right, lock the cameras off and let the person do the moving. It is possible to pan and zoom when using CSO, but since both cameras have to move at exactly the same time it's a very difficult thing to do successfully and you would be well advised not to try it unless you have a lot of rehearsal time at your disposal. Even cutting to a close-up of your person involves changing the shot on both cameras and this again can take time.

CSO is in fact a very time-consuming process altogether, but don't be too put off – the effect can be spectacular. The most common use of CSO is of course to provide a magic window for the news but it is also the basis of most shots which set viewers buzzing with the question 'How did they do that?' So it's certainly worth exploring further – this Briefing is merely a short introduction to a big subject which can become very complicated and intriguing.

SUMMARY BRIEFING NUMBER THREE

Chromakey

Chromakey, also known as colour separation overlay or
CSO, is a sort of electronic scissors which cuts out all the
parts you don't want from one picture (colour them blue)
and superimposes the remainder on another picture.

Your background picture can come from any source. If you
are going for realism choose a background which has some
depth in it.

Your foreground can be anything or anyone provided it isn't
blue (if you are using blue as your CSO colour). To give the
illusion of depth it's a good idea to have some props in the
foreground set which match those in the background
picture. Matching the lighting in both pictures can be difficult.

You can use any colour you want as your CSO colour. Blue
is most commonly used because it is hardly present at all in
human skin tones.

The CSO colour can come from paint, light or cloth. Make
sure blue light doesn't spill onto your foreground figures.

For very long shots cut down the area of the studio you need
to colour blue by giving the foreground camera a 'vignette'
to shoot through.

Camera movements with CSO are difficult to do
successfully. Try to avoid them unless you have lots of
rehearsal time. Also keep the number of different shots to a
minimum as each shot can take a long time to set up.

CSO effects can be spectacular and are well worth exploring.

Don't be frightened to use CSO.

Briefing Number Four
Negative and Reversal Film

There are two types of film: negative and reversal. The procedures for using them are rather different.

A *NEGATIVE*
Negative is used as follows:

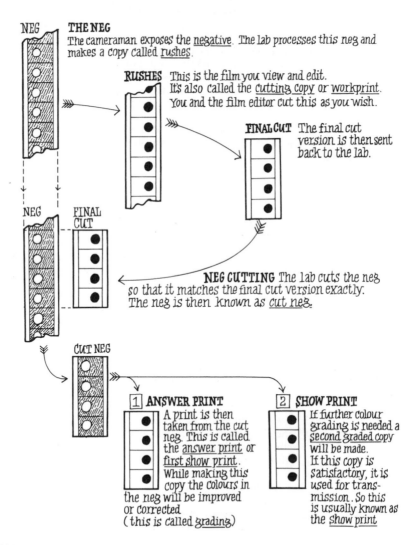

NEG

THE NEG
The cameraman exposes the <u>negative</u>. The lab processes this neg and makes a copy called <u>rushes</u>.

RUSHES This is the film you view and edit. It's also called the <u>cutting copy</u> or <u>workprint</u>. You and the film editor cut this as you wish.

FINAL CUT The final cut version is then sent back to the lab.

NEG **FINAL CUT**

NEG CUTTING The lab cuts the neg so that it matches the final cut version exactly. The neg is then known as <u>cut neg</u>.

CUT NEG

1 **ANSWER PRINT**
A print is then taken from the cut neg. This is called the <u>answer print</u> or <u>first show print</u>. While making this copy the colours in the neg will be improved or corrected (this is called <u>grading</u>)

2 **SHOW PRINT**
If further colour grading is needed a <u>second graded copy</u> will be made. If this copy is satisfactory, it is used for transmission. So this is usually known as the <u>show print</u>

You should allow several days after your final cut version is ready for the laboratory to cut the negative, grade the colours and produce a show print. So obviously negative is not recommended for film (such as news film) which has to be transmitted as quickly as possible. In exceptional circumstances you can in fact transmit the negative directly, but this is not advised as there is a high risk of damage to the fragile material during editing and transmission.

B   *REVERSAL*
Reversal film can either be transmitted directly or copied.

(i)   *Transmitting the Master*
The direct transmission method is straightforward:

The film the cameraman exposes and sends to the laboratory is called the master (or camera original) and is the film which is transmitted.

advantages of transmitting the master

Transmitting the master gives you two important advantages. The first is of course speed. The processing time for reversal can be less than 15 minutes plus the time it takes for the film to run through the machines (which depends on how fast the machines are running). A good news laboratory should be able to process a 400-foot (122-metre) roll in under half an hour, if you are really in a hurry.

The other advantage of transmitting the master is cost. As only one piece of film goes through the laboratory only once, costs are kept to the minimum.

disadvantages of transmitting the master

There are of course disadvantages as well. As you are transmitting the actual piece of film exposed by the cameraman there is no opportunity for the laboratory to grade the colours and improve the picture. If you shorten the shot while editing and then decide to lengthen it again, the picture will jump slightly at the point where the shot was cut. And inevitably reversal film collects dirt and scratches during editing, even if it is carefully handled.

(ii)   *Copying Reversal*
The disadvantages of transmitting the master directly can be avoided if you first make a copy of it. You then use this copy as a cutting copy, cut the master to match the final cut

155

version and transmit the master which has thus been spared the wear and tear of editing.

Or if time and cost permit, when you have edited the cutting copy and cut the master to match, ask the laboratory to make a fully corrected show print from the master. This show print will have graded colours and will be free of joins. It can also include mixes, superimposed titles and other special effects just like a show print made from negative. It is at this stage, by the way, that an optical sound track can be added if needed.

There are two ways of making a copy from reversal:

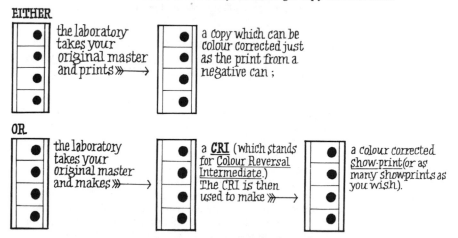

EITHER

the laboratory takes your original master and prints »——→

a copy which can be colour corrected just as the print from a negative can ;

OR

the laboratory takes your original master and makes »——→

a **CRI** (which stands for Colour Reversal Intermediate.) The CRI is then used to make »——→

a colour corrected show-print (or as many showprints as you wish).

The advantage of making a copy directly from the master is that it is faster and cheaper. But if you want several copies, the wear and tear on your master may become serious and so going through a colour reversal intermediate is preferable. You should note, however, that it may not be possible to insert shots from a copy made directly from the master into the original master, because the emulsion (the side of the film containing the picture) will not be on the same side and some of the pictures will therefore appear blurred on the screen. The same may also be true sometimes with shots from a copy made via a CRI. This problem of making sure the emulsion is on the right side is complicated and you should leave it to your film editor to sort out. (You can tell which side of the film the emulsion is on, by the way, because the emulsion side is less shiny and will stick to a moistened finger.)

keeping reversal and neg clean

If you are using the direct transmission method, it's difficult to keep your reversal master clean and free from scratches, however carefully it is handled. This is particularly true if you are going to be editing for more than a day or two. If your film is at all precious or unrepeatable, it's a good idea to have a copy of it made on videotape while the master is still in good condition; you should do this even before you send the master off to the laboratory for copying.

Keeping negative clean is not as great a problem, since you use the cutting copy for editing and the master negative is never handled at all outside the dustfree conditions of the laboratory and the neg cutting room. If dirt does get onto the negative, it's particularly annoying as it shows up as a white spot on the print. On reversal dirt shows up black and this is less noticeable.

negative or reversal? So which type of film should you use: negative or reversal? The answer depends on what sort of film you are making and how much time and money your station is willing to spend on achieving quality.

For short magazine items and films which have to be finished in a few days, reversal is clearly the winner. If it's exposed correctly, the quality should be almost as good as negative; if you make a copy using the CRI procedure the laboratory will have a chance to correct the colours. If it's not exposed correctly (particularly if it's over-exposed) and you aren't making a copy, you will have to rely on the electronic colour corrections which can be made during transmission (though these can be a little hit-and-miss unless there is time for a proper rehearsal). But perhaps the biggest drawback of reversal is that by the time your film arrives in the library it will be very much the worse for wear. So a station which uses nothing but reversal film never really manages to build up a good-quality film library.

Negative film, on the other hand, is the better film to choose if you are working on a major programme and will have lots of time for editing. The laboratory procedure is designed more for quality than for speed or economy, and the definition of pictures on negative is better, giving you better quality copies (copies from reversal can be a little fuzzy).

But in the end it all boils down to one thing: money. A film shot on negative costs about three times as much as a film using a single reversal master for shooting, editing and transmission. Is the extra cost justified for your programme?

SUMMARY BRIEFING NUMBER FOUR

Negative and Reversal Film

The procedure for *negative:*

– the cameraman exposes the *neg*

– the lab prints *rushes*

– you edit the rushes till you have a *final cut version*

– the lab cuts the neg to match your final cut

– and then prints a colour-corrected *answer print*

– if further corrections are needed, the lab makes a *show print*

– either the answer print or the show print is used for transmission.

The procedure for *reversal:*

either you edit and transmit the master

or you copy the master (directly or via a colour reversal intermediate), cut the copy, cut the master reversal to match and then transmit the master,

or when you have edited the cutting copy and the master to match, you make a second copy from the master.

Dirt on reversal shows up black on the screen.

Dirt from negative shows up white on the screen and is more noticeable (but easier to avoid).

Advantages of *reversal:*

– fast

– cheap

– good quality if handled well.

Disadvantages of *reversal:*

– if you transmit the master you can't improve colours (except by more hit-and-miss electronic means)

– picture will jump if you shorten a shot and then decide to lengthen it again

– it's difficult to keep reversal free from dust and scratches.

The last two disadvantages can be avoided by making a copy of the master. But remember that you can't always mix shots from copies with shots from the master.

Advantages of *negative:*

– picture quality is given priority over speed and economy

– the pictures are more distinct and so copy better

– the negative is hardly handled at all and so can be used to build up a good quality film library.

Disadvantages of *negative:*

– more time

– more money.

Use reversal for short magazine items and films in a hurry.

Use negative for major programmes and films which will have lots of time in the editing room.

Briefing Number Five
Lighting

If you had to choose the single most important thing about pictures you would be well advised to choose light. Because pictures *are* light. Video and film cameras are simply ways of capturing light, television transmitters are a way of distributing light and the television set is a way of reproducing light. So as a television producer you have to be aware of light, because that is ultimately the stuff in which you are dealing.

It's a pity therefore – as light is so central a requirement – that television is not happy with most of the light which surrounds us every day. Our eyes are more sensitive and – aided by our brain – more selective than the television camera. Most indoor lighting, for example, has been designed for the human eye and not the camera and so looks unsatisfactory on television (you can see how unsatisfactory by half-closing your eyes). For the same reason most landscapes look flat and disappointing on television: sunlight is not designed for the camera and you can't help out nature by relighting a whole landscape. When you are faced with this sort of problem, try speaking nicely to the cameraman to see if he wouldn't mind getting up early next morning for the shot – the dawn light will make the view so much more interesting on camera . . .

For most indoor locations, however, you are very much in the business of modifying what light you find to make it look better on television. The situation you will come across most often is the basic one-camera interview. The simplest way to light the interviewee is to shine a light straight at him from the front, rather like a fixed flash bulb on a stills camera. The result is pure Totter: a washed-out face devoid of detail with a thick black shadow on the wall behind. News editors sometimes have to accept this sort of picture for their bulletins but they should do so only reluctantly and then ask questions. Other producers should never accept it at all.

No, there is more to lighting than just providing enough to record a picture. It's also an art, and it's very much the art of the cameraman. In fact not so long ago the chief cameraman on big productions for the cinema was usually known as the lighting cameraman – that shows you how important the real craftsmen think lighting is. So once you have discussed with the cameraman where you want to do your interview and told him of any special points which might affect the lighting

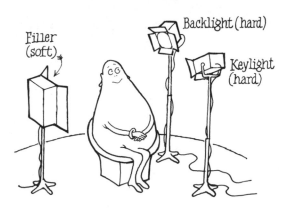

Filler (soft)

Backlight (hard)

Keylight (hard)

Lighting an interview

(a particular mood you want to establish, perhaps), let him get on with it.

lighting an interview

While this is going on, it won't hurt you to learn a little about the usual approach to lighting an interview. This is to use three lights: a key light, a filler and a back light. The key light is placed in front of the interviewee on the same side of the camera to which he is looking (this minimises the shadow from the nose). It shines down on him but from not too high up (watch those shadows under the eyebrows) and it's usually a hard light (which casts distinct shadows) emphasising the features of the face. The side of the face furthest from the key light will now be comparatively dark – this is where the filler comes in. It is directed towards the dark side of the interviewee's face in order to lift the light level on this side of the face without casting any hard shadows. So the filler is a soft light (one which casts very soft, indistinct shadows). The back light is then placed to one side and behind the interviewee to make him stand out from the background and give a little extra sparkle to his hair. Usually the back light is also a hard light.

This is the usual approach to lighting an interview but there are almost as many variations as there are cameramen. Some cameramen use hard lights only, some like to bounce lights off the walls and ceilings, some cameramen take white umbrellas on location to act as portable light reflectors. But all these approaches are relatives (though admittedly some are extremely distant relatives) of the basic key/filler/back combination.

Your job is to decide whether you like the lighting and whether it fulfils your requirements. The best way of doing this is to think about what lighting can contribute to the picture.

161

Lighting Brings out Highlights
The viewer's eye is attracted to the lightest part of the
picture first. So make sure that's where your main point of
interest is and that there isn't too much competition from
other bright patches of light. Sometimes in entertainment
programmes one sees a set decorated with lights which flash
so brightly that they constantly draw the viewer's attention
away from the artist. From the artist's point of view it's like
trying to upstage a lighthouse at night – he hasn't a chance.
Lighting should always draw attention to your artist, not
outshine him.

Lighting Sets the Mood
Bright lights make people happy, gloom makes people feel
subdued. Think of fireworks and public illuminations at
times of celebration, sunset when everything slows down,
the dead of night when danger lurks. Clearly people are very
influenced by light. You can profit from this, as it provides
you with a second short cut to the viewer's feelings (the first
short cut is music). So try and define what element in the
scene you want to emphasise; in a location interview, for
example, you may want to highlight an official's business-
like approach to problems (brighter light called for) or his
sympathetic consideration of the public's best interests
(obviously more gentle lighting would be suitable). Look at
the lines on the interviewee's face: do you want to make
something of them or smooth them out? It's all done by
lighting.

Lighting Gives Depth
The television screen is two-dimensional; life is three-
dimensional. Careful lighting helps restore the third
dimension to television. If you light the background of the
shot as brightly as the interviewee in the foreground, he will
look like a cardboard cut-out stuck on a postcard. Reduce
the lighting on the back wall a little and immediately your
subject stops looking like a cut-out and starts looking like a
three-dimensional person. Good lighting has given depth to
the picture.

the source of light
There are occasions when the highlights, mood and depth
seem fine but something still isn't quite right about the
picture. This is the time to think about the source of your
light.

When you are out of doors, the sun is the source of light and
you have one shadow. When you are indoors, there may be
several sources giving you several shadows and if they all
appear to be equally important, the effect can be rather
messy. So discuss with the cameraman where the best place

for the main source of light would be. If you have an obvious light source in the picture (like a window or a standard lamp) the lighting which the cameraman has arranged should appear to come from these visible sources; in other words the side of the face farthest away from the window or the lamp should appear to be less brightly lit. The viewer then sees that the lighting has an apparent source and it makes sense and will appear right. If you don't have an obvious light source in the picture, you are free to pick whatever direction you want for your apparent source of light. The point is that light usually comes from somewhere (not everywhere) and to make your picture look realistic you have to choose an apparent source for it, even though it is in fact coming from lots of different directions.

Mixed Light

Daylight is bluish, artificial light is yellowish. If you have an indoor scene which combines direct daylight with artificial light, the colours will be distorted on television, unless the cameraman takes steps to correct for it.

He usually does this by putting blue filters on the lamps so that the artificial light now matches the bluish daylight (your eyes won't notice much difference, but the camera will). Putting filters on is not difficult to do, but it does take a little time and cuts the amount of light coming from the lamps. This in turn restricts the area you can light effectively. Alternatively the cameraman can filter the daylight by putting orange filters on the windows, but this again takes time and lowers the general light level.

So if you're in a hurry it's quite a good idea to find a way round the mixed light problem. The most usual dodge is to draw the curtains or drop the blind, thus excluding direct daylight from the room and the picture. Or you can move your scene into a corner of the room without a window.

studio lighting

Studio lighting is at once easier and more difficult than lighting on location. It's easier because the average television studio has a large number of lights available (on location the biggest problem is usually that you don't have enough). It's more difficult because most work in the studio is done in a continuous sequence and so you can't reset the lights for each shot.

Most studio lighting therefore has to be a compromise between the demands of different cameras. You the producer can help by keeping your artists away from back walls and overhanging bits of scenery (these always cause shadow problems); by leaving room for the sound boom

163

under soft lights (again to lessen shadow problems); by making sure that the sets are not too cramped to be lit; by being able to discuss the problems in detail with the lighting supervisor at the planning meeting; and above all by knowing what you want from the lighting.

This really is the key to lighting: knowing what you want. The best way of doing this is to get into the habit of looking at the light around you – outdoors and indoors, at dawn, dusk and noon, on sunny days and cloudy days and days which are not quite either. Half close your eyes to see how much detail the camera would miss. Think about what the light is doing to the scene in front of you and how the scene would change if the light changed. Don't forget to look at the light in other programmes and films, in photographs and paintings. And don't forget also to look at the shadows – they contribute creatively as much as the light. The art of lighting for the camera is also the art of shadows.

SUMMARY BRIEFING NUMBER FIVE

Lighting

Normal everyday light is OK for eyes, not so good for TV. You have to accept normal light outdoors. Indoors you can and should modify the available light.

Interviews are usually lit using

– a key light (hard) to bring out facial features

– a filler (soft) to lift the light level on the side of the face furthest from the key

– a back light (hard) to give depth and add sparkle to the hair.

Check lighting by considering

– highlights: does the lighting draw the viewer's attention to where you want it?

– mood: does the lighting hit the right note?

– depth: does the lighting make your picture 3D?

– source: does the lighting have an apparent source?

Mixed Light

Daylight is bluish, artificial light is yellowish. If you have mixed light in your scene the cameraman will have to fix filters on the lamps or over the windows. This takes time, cuts light output and restricts the area which can be lit. You can avoid this by drawing the curtains or moving the scene away from the window.

Studio Lighting

Studio lighting has to be planned in great detail because there isn't time to reset the lighting between each shot. Help the lighting supervisor by

– keeping artists away from back walls and overhangs

– leaving room for the sound boom under soft lights

– ensuring sets are not too cramped

– giving a full briefing at the planning meeting

– knowing what you want.

Learn to appreciate light by observing it (and the shadows it throws).

Briefing Number Six
Sound

Close your eyes and listen to the sounds around you. First listen to the loudest noises and think where they are coming from. Then try and disregard them and listen out for the most distant sound which you can hear (birds? traffic? aircraft?). Then after a while come in closer and concentrate on the sounds immediately round you (radio or TV sets? a breeze blowing? people talking? clocks ticking?). Finally try and shut out all these sounds and listen to your own body. Can you hear yourself breathe?

You have just done what no microphone can do: that is, choose the sounds you wish to hear. Your ears, like your eyes, can be directed by the brain to concentrate on certain things and disregard others (think how you can select the voice of just one person talking to you from the hubbub of voices at a crowded party). Microphones, on the other hand, are more like fishing nets. They scoop up all the sound which falls within their range.

So mikes have to be chosen carefully for your programme. This is really the job of the sound engineer, who knows the shape and size of each microphone's net.

microphone ranges Some mikes will net sound from all sides – they are known as omnidirectional. Others will net sound coming from anywhere in front. Others will net sound coming from both in front and behind – they are known as mikes with a figure-of-eight response. And the gun mike, probably the one most commonly used outside the studio, nets sound only from the direction in which it is pointed.

All this lies within the speciality of the sound engineer. What you have to decide and tell him is what you want to hear. When recording an interview on location do you want to hear the interviewer's questions or will you be replacing them with commentary later? Or in the case of a musical show, how much of the studio audience's applause do you want to hear?

gun mikes Some mikes have particular advantages and disadvantages which you should be aware of. The gun mike is marvellous for excluding unwanted noise. But it is also so narrowly directional that if it isn't pointed exactly at what you want to hear (your interviewee, for example) it will give you a usable recording only of background noise (the busy road behind).

neck mikes

The lanyard or neck mike (also known as a 'lavalier' after Madame de la Vallière, a mistress of the French king, Louis the Fourteenth, who was famed for her neck jewellery) is fine for static interviews, but can pick up a disturbing amount of rustling from clothes if the wearer moves around too much. The lanyard (the cord which goes round the neck) and the mike cable should be tucked away out of sight of the camera. But if you want your interviewee to be able to move around, it's best to use a gun mike on location and a mike on an overhead boom in the studio.

hand mikes

Hand-held microphones also give people more freedom to move around but you should let people rehearse with them before using them in front of the camera. Hand mikes often pick up sound from a very small area only and it takes a few minutes' practice to find the best place to hold them and the best way of managing the cable.

radio mikes

The radio mike gives the greatest freedom of movement. The mike comes with a tiny transmitter which the user hides in his pocket; he can then wander around wherever he wants within the range of the transmitter and without any cables dangling behind him. Radio mikes are equally effective in the studio or on location. But sometimes they are impossible to use near military bases or airports because of other traffic on the frequencies they use.

sound perspective

Radio mikes raise another feature about sound which it is worth thinking about – the perspective of sound. With a radio mike it is possible to see a person in long shot and hear him in close-up (as clearly as you would with your ear to his chest). Obviously if you are taping or filming someone climbing a cliff, this effect can be very dramatic. But what of a person shouting for help in a large deserted warehouse? Do you want to hear his voice close-up or echoing in the distance? There are no rules about which option is better. But don't forget that in most situations you have a choice of sound perspectives and you can use them to your advantage.

mikes in shot

In practice a large proportion of the time you spend thinking about sound will be taken up worrying about something far less artistic than sound perspectives, but something just as important: the problem of keeping mikes and mike shadows out of the picture. There are rigid conventions about which mikes are acceptable in shot and which aren't. Mikes on stands (either on tables or on the floor), hand-held mikes, and (more recently) lapel mikes which clip on to clothing are acceptable. Other mikes are not. Making sure that the sound recordist can get in close enough without having the mike or its shadow actually in the picture can be surprisingly complicated. Don't worry if the mike keeps dipping in and out of shot while you are setting up a shot on location or in the studio. It's just the sound recordist establishing how close he can get the mike without it being seen on camera. But if the mike is still in shot when you are about to start recording, ask the sound recordist if he has a problem.

wild tracks

Finally, a point about recording sound 'wild' (that is, without running the camera). Make sure that your sound man records at least a minute of the background sound on each location you visit – the editor needs this to cover any awkward gaps in the synchronised sound track. Every location has its own distinct sound and it takes far less time to record it on the spot than try and find something in the library later. Even quiet locations like museums and sound studios have their own distinct sound signature.

SUMMARY BRIEFING NUMBER SIX

Sound

Microphones can't choose what sounds they pick up. But the shape and size of their net varies. Help the sound engineer choose the right mike for the job by telling him clearly what you want to hear.

Gun mikes have to be pointed accurately.

Neck mikes are noisy if the wearer moves around too much.

Hand-held mikes need practice to be used successfully.

Radio mikes give great freedom of movement.

Don't forget sound perspective can be used to your advantage.

Keeping mikes and mike shadows out of shot can be tricky.

Record one minute wild track on each location.

Briefing Number Seven
Lenses

Zooms

The zoom lens is the lens most commonly found on television cameras, both film and video. It offers the advantages of a whole set of lenses because of its ability to change its focal length to order.

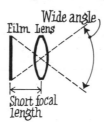 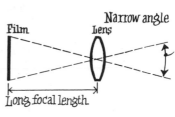

focal lengths and angles of view

The focal length is the distance between the lens and the film (or in the case of a video camera between the lens and the camera tubes or tube). You can see from the diagram that the shorter the focal length, the wider the angle of view.

Zoom lenses are often described by the ratio between their widest and narrowest angles: thus a lens with a wide angle of 50° and a narrow angle of 5° is a 10 : 1 zoom (you say 'ten to one' zoom).

With a film camera it is more usual to talk about the focal length rather than the angle of view, but the principle is the same. So a zoom lens with a short focal length of 12 mm (millimetres) and a long focal length of 120 mm is also known as a 10 : 1 zoom (though logically one should perhaps say 1 : 10). You can get zoom lenses in a variety of short and long (or wide and narrow) combinations – anything from 6 : 1 to 20 : 1.

making use of lens distortion

So what use can you make of this information about zoom lenses? The first point to realise is that zoom lenses distort the picture at both ends of the zoom. The picture is most natural in the central areas of the zoom. At the wide-angle end the zoom makes the foreground and background look further apart than they really are, and the speed of something moving towards or away from the camera is exaggerated. At the narrow-angle end of the lens the effect is like looking through a telescope: you only see a very small part of the complete scene and the foreground and background seem very close together, giving the picture a

169

rather flat appearance and making movement towards or away from the camera appear very slow. The background is also out of focus. You can use these effects to your advantage by filming, for example, a distant runner coming towards you on the narrow end of the zoom – the flattening effect of the lens will make him appear to be running on the spot and will concentrate the viewer's attention very attractively on the effort he is putting into his running. But make sure that the camera is on a tripod: at the narrow end of the zoom the tiniest tremble on the camera turns into huge wobbles on the picture.

The Difference Between a Track and a Zoom
The picture of the man appearing to run on the spot is the key to understanding the difference between a track and a zoom. The zoom lens gives you a closer shot by narrowing its angle of view; the track gives you a closer shot by moving the camera in closer without changing the angle of view of the lens. So the zoom makes thing flatter, puts the background out of focus and slows down movement towards and away from the camera (as described above). The track makes things seem further apart, as the closer you get to two objects, the further apart they seem. As a result movement towards and away from the camera seems faster.

The difference between a
Zoom and a Track

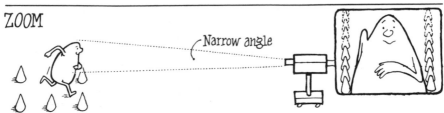

ZOOM

Narrow angle

END·OF·ZOOM SHOT : Running on spot. Background out of focus. Flat picture. Note position of cones.

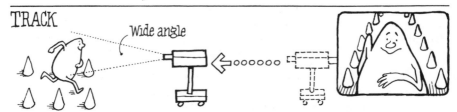

TRACK

Wide angle

SHOT AFTER TRACKING IN CAMERA : Runner comes through shot and past camera more quickly. Picture has more depth. Foreground and background are in focus. Compare position of cones with end-of-zoom shot.

'Macro' Close-ups and Diopters

The normal zoom lens fitted to most cameras will probably give you close-ups as big as you need; most of them can fill the screen with a matchbox. But if you want a close-up of something really small (like filling the screen with the picture on the matchbox) you may not be able to go in close enough without losing focus.

With video the 'macro' close-up facility on most cameras should get you the shot you want. With film you should ask for a diopter lens, an attachment which fits on to the front of the zoom and allows you to go in very tight and stay in focus. It takes a few minutes to set up but it is worth the trouble if you want the shot.

Other Lenses

the wide-angle lens

The versatility of the zoom will give you all the shots you need for most everyday programmes but it's worth checking what other lenses your camera department has available. Wide-angle lenses (with a short focal length) can give you a very effective shot in confined spaces (a small kitchen, for example) and can also give impressive results in landscapes or looking up at tall buildings. The wider the lens, the more it tends to distort the picture round the edges – this is particularly noticeable when you introduce a camera movement into the shot, but the effect can be interesting. Another advantage of the wide-angle is that it is usually more efficient than a narrow-angle lens at transmitting light into the camera; it is what is known as a 'fast' lens. So in situations where the light is too low for the zoom (where the zoom is too 'slow') the wide-angle lens can sometimes give you an acceptable picture.

telephoto

At the other end of the scale there are telephoto lenses of various sizes, some of them so long that they have a little bracket of their own to support them. These long lenses, with a focal length of anything from 200 mm to 1000 mm and more, are often difficult to use. They are less efficient at transmitting light into the camera (in other words they are 'slow' lenses) and therefore need a bright day before they can be taken out. But if it is hot, heat haze can obscure the picture badly; although the effect can be attractive for a shot or two it soon becomes tiresome. The tiniest breeze can also cause the lens to tremble, which gives the picture an exaggerated wobble. Altogether telephoto lenses are for locations where you are not in a hurry.

F-numbers and the Depth of Field

The final thing you should know about lenses is what the f-number is and its relationship with the depth of field.

Think of the lens as the window of a small room (there is only one window in the room.) It's obvious that the bigger the window is, the more light will enter the room. As we have seen, all lenses have a focal length – as far as our room is concerned, the focal length would be the distance between the window and the wall facing the window.

If you wanted a way of comparing how well lenses when fully open transmit light into the camera (in other words, you wanted to know the *speed* of the lens), you could do so by working out the ratio of the size of each lens to its focal length (the ratio of the size of the fully opened window to the distance between it and the wall opposite). So if a lens is 25 mm across and has a focal length of 70 mm we would say it has a ratio of 25 : 70 which equals 1 : 2.8 (divide both sides by 25). This ratio of 1 : 2.8 is in fact the f-number of this particular lens when fully open and you will see it written on the side of the lens (usually as f2.8). This is about the normal speed for a standard lens; telephotos are often much slower, wide-angles usually faster. You can buy special lenses which are very fast indeed but they cost a lot. Generally speaking the faster the lens, the more it costs.

The f-number is also known as the 'lens aperture ratio' or 'aperture' for short ('aperture' means 'opening'). Many lenses also have a 'T-number' written on the side which tells the cameraman how efficiently this particular lens transmits light – there is always a slight variation, even with lenses of identical design.

F-Number Settings
F-number settings (or aperture settings) are usually arranged so that each setting reduces the amount of light entering the lens to about half that of the previous setting.

f-number	1.4	2	2.8	4	5.6	8	11	16
amount of light entering lens	1	$\frac{1}{2}$	$\frac{1}{4}$	$\frac{1}{8}$	$\frac{1}{16}$	$\frac{1}{32}$	$\frac{1}{64}$	$\frac{1}{128}$

So the light entering the lens at a setting of f2 is $\frac{1}{2}$ that at a setting of f1.4.

---

throwing focus

The cameraman can alter the f-number of a lens to increase or reduce the amount of light it transmits into the camera – he will usually refer to this as 'changing the stop'. This need not concern you particularly except that you should realise that the lower the f-number, the shallower is the area of the picture in which everything will be in sharp focus. This applies particularly to film cameras; modern video cameras

Throwing Focus

Focus on Boy......throw focus to.......Teacher

electronically sharpen any edges they see and so the effect is less noticeable.

depth of field

This area where everything is in focus in the shot is known as the depth of field. You are more likely to come up against a narrow depth of field because you are using the narrow-angle end of the zoom than because of a low f-number. But fear not, you can sometimes use a narrow depth of field to do what is known as 'throw focus' or 'pull focus'. Supposing you have a close-up of a schoolboy lighting a cigarette. Behind him the picture is just a blur. The cameraman suddenly throws focus from the profile of the boy in the front to the blur in the background, which sharpens into a picture of a disapproving teacher . . . It can be a dramatic effect.

SUMMARY BRIEFING NUMBER SEVEN

Lenses

Zooms

The zoom lens is the most useful lens because it can change its focal length to order.

The shorter the focal length, the wider the angle of view.

The longer the focal length, the narrower the angle of view.

Zoom lenses are described by the ratio of their widest to their narrowest angle. Thus a lens with a wide angle of 50° and a narrow angle of 5° is known as a 10 : 1 zoom (a 'ten-to-one' zoom).

Zoom lenses give their most natural picture in the central part of the zoom. At the wide-angle end

– the distance between foreground and background is exaggerated

---

– the speed of anything moving towards or away from the camera is exaggerated.

At the narrow-angle end

– you see only a small part of the picture (like looking through a telescope)

– the picture appears flat

– movement towards or away from the camera is very slow

– the background is out of focus.

Use these narrow-angle effects to your advantage (the shot of the approaching runner). But make sure the cameraman is using a tripod.

Difference between a Track and a Zoom

The zoom is giving you a small part of the picture with all the narrow-angle distortions mentioned above.

The track distorts things less. Things seem further apart when you move the camera in closer.

Macro Close-ups and Diopters

Use to get in really close to small objects without losing focus.

Other Lenses

Wide-angle lenses distort round the edges. Camera movement draws attention to this distortion, but it can be interesting. Wide-angles transmit light well and can sometimes give you an acceptable picture when light is too low for the zoom.

Telephoto lenses need good light, no wind and not too much heat haze.

F-numbers and the Depth of Field

The f-number or lens aperture ratio is the ratio of the size of the lens to its focal length.

The f-number of the lens when fully open is known as the speed of the lens. The higher the f-number, the greater the depth of field (the area where everything is in sharp focus).

The lower the f-number, the shallower the depth of field. The depth of field also narrows with the angle of vision. You can use this to your advantage by 'throwing' or 'pulling' focus.

Briefing Number Eight
Clapper Board Conventions

You should always use a clapper board when shooting.
Even if you are not recording sound, or are using video or
commag film (where the sound is recorded on the film itself
and is therefore always in sync) – on such occasions you
should put one clapper on the front of each tape or roll and a
clapper on the front of each shot.

Because the first function of the clapper is to identify
shots for when you are editing (being able to pick out the
beginnings and endings of shots while spooling through film
or video at high speed saves a lot of time). The second
function is of course to provide a sync point for sepmag
sound recording.

Here are the different ways of using the clapper.

For each Sync Shot
Hold the clapper in front of the camera, read out the shot
and take number and drop the clapper arm. If you are using
the clapper to identify shots on video or commag you don't
need to drop the clapper arm. Though some directors prefer
to do so, as it concentrates the mind of everyone most
wonderfully. Don't clap the board in people's faces – it isn't
polite and doesn't help their nerves.

End Board
If you don't put the clapper on at the beginning of the shot,
put it on at the end – but upside down. Don't forget to say
'End board'. Use end boards when shooting people (or
animals) who might be disconcerted by a clapper at the
beginning of the shot.

Note that end boards take the film editor longer to sync up (he has to run through the film three times instead of one). So don't use them too often.

Sync to Second Clap
If for some reason camera or sound miss the first clap they may ask to do it again. Read out the shot and take number and then say 'Sync to second clap'.

Mute Film
If not recording sync sound, hold the board open in front of camera without clapping. One board will do for a group of consecutive mute shots.

Mute End Boards

Use the same procedure as for mute film, but hold the board upside down.

Mike Tap

On some formal occasions (during a speech or religious service for example) it may not be possible to use the clapper board without interrupting the proceedings. But you will still want sync sound and the editor will need a sync point.

On these occasions use a mike tap. Pan the camera to the sound man (or get him to walk into the shot) and ask him to tap the mike. This will make a noise on the sound track which the editor can use to sync with the film.

SUMMARY BRIEFING NUMBER EIGHT

Clapper Board Conventions

Use the clapper board

– to identify all shots and rolls

– to provide a sync point for the film editor.

For normal shots read out shot and take number, then clap (clap not needed for video and commag).

For end board claps, hold the board upside down.

For mute shots, don't clap the board.

Use mike taps when you can't use the clapper board.

Briefing Number Nine
Vox Pops

What do the people think?

It's a question which should crop up fairly regularly in
television production offices, if only to remind programme-
makers that viewers are people and public opinion is
therefore important.

What about including some public opinion in the
programme? Actually letting the public have a say? It would
certainly make a refreshing change after all those experts
and officials.

But how to do it – interview a spokesman? Interview several
spokesmen? But interviews eat up television time, more
time than there is available, don't they . . . ?

At times like this you should turn to the technique of the vox
pop. Vox pop stands for *vox populi* which is Latin for *the
voice of the people*. The recipe is as follows: decide on the
question you want to ask (should old people be given free
bus passes? what do you think of miniskirts? do we have too
many public holidays?); go out on the street with a camera
crew and put your question to about ten people (choose
women as well as men, young and old as well as middle-
aged); then edit all the answers together. And that's a vox
pop.

The editing is important. You don't need to use the question
more than once in the finished programme and you don't
need to run all the answers at full length. Instead, look at the
answers very carefully and pick out the heart of them only –
at most two or three sentences, sometimes as little as two or
three words. This is really very important; the better the
pruning, the more powerful the vox pop. It's not very
difficult, as you don't have to worry about continuity or
cutaways. Notice you don't have to film any cutaways; you
can just cut straight from one person to the next.

Of course you don't have to show all the interviews you shot
or show them in the order in which you shot them.
Assemble them instead so that each one makes its neighbour
more effective and don't forget to keep a good one for the
end. Some producers like to make sure that each contributor
to the vox pop looks to the other side of camera from the
previous one (so that the answers go cam. left, cam. right,

cam. left, cam. right and so on). But I think it is far more important to let the content of the answers dictate the assembly order.

When you are interviewing for a vox pop you can of course rephrase the question as you wish. If the first answer is not very good, put the question in another way; it's your job to get a quotable answer and sometimes you may have to go on with one interviewee for quite a time before you get it. This is especially true when you are talking to children.

If you are talking to a group of people and a lot of them answer at once, pick one to talk to first, tell the camera and sound man who it is and then wait till they have found him and are focused on him before you start. Camera and sound will need a few seconds to move to each new contributor; if you jump from person to person they won't be able to follow you.

And that really is all there is to the vox pop. It's a nice simple technique which if done well can give you lively 1½ to 2 minutes of programme. Don't make it longer, as one of the great assets of the vox pop is that it can provide a change of pace from the other sequences. The vox pop can of course tackle serious subjects (like refugees) but it is more often used for its entertainment value – at least one very popular programme on British television owes a great deal of its success to the laughs it gets from its regular vox pop.

SUMMARY BRIEFING NUMBER NINE

Vox Pops

Let a range of people have their say by asking about ten people the same question and cutting together the core of each answer. Include the question only once in the finished programme and cut the answers very severely to give pace to the vox pop.

When interviewing contributors, rephrase the question if necessary to get a good answer.

If talking to a group of people, give camera and sound time to focus on each contributor.

Vox pops can be used for serious as well as light-hearted programmes.

Briefing Number Ten
Statements to Camera

The statement to camera (or piece to camera, or stand-upper, as it is also known) should on the whole be tackled only by professional television reporters or presenters.

It's a useful method of getting non-visual information over to the audience in a direct way and the evidence in the picture that the reporter/presenter is 'on the spot' adds enormously both to his authority and the viewer's inclination to listen to him.

It follows therefore that either the background in the shot should be identifiable, or that the reporter should refer to the location in his piece. If the location is an unfamiliar one, why not start with a long shot showing the reporter in the location and then cut to a mid-shot of the reporter while he is talking (remember to shoot a good overlap on the two takes)? Or pan off the scene on to the reporter as he starts talking? Or let the reporter walk into shot as he delivers his piece? Or start on a close-up and throw focus to the reporter in the background?

There are many possible variations – the statement to camera does not always have to be a static shot with a reporter just standing there in front of some scene. If you want some ideas, watch how the statement to camera is handled in major documentary series like 'Life on Earth' and 'The Ascent of Man'.

Two points to look out for. Firstly, the authority of the statement is seriously weakened if the reporter has to refer to notes. If the reporter finds it difficult to deliver the whole statement from memory you should shorten it, or record it in two shots, or hold up a prompt board behind the camera with notes on it (any large piece of cardboard or stiff paper will do). Some reporters hang their script below the camera lens with a piece of sticky tape, which works quite well provided the reporter isn't short-sighted. Anything is better than the pause on camera while the reporter consults notes held in his hand. The only exception is when the reporter has to quote some precise figures which he can't be expected to remember; on such occasions reading the numbers from notes in his hand adds to his authority.

The second point concerns mikes. It's not really necessary to have a mike in shot at all but many reporters seem to gain confidence from clutching their symbol of office. If that is so, make sure the mike is a good-looking one – there really is no need nowadays for reporters to brandish one of those enormous iron lollipops with a dirty piece of foam on top of it. Especially if the reporter is a delicate and nicely dressed lady . . .

SUMMARY BRIEFING NUMBER TEN

Statements to Camera

In the hands of a professional reporter the statement to camera is a good way of delivering non-visual information directly to the viewer.

Being on the spot gives the reporter authority.

Statements don't all have to be one static shot. Try

– a long shot followed by a mid-shot (remember overlaps)

– a pan to the reporter (cue him to start speaking at the start of the pan)

– letting the reporter walk into shot

– throwing focus to the reporter.

If the reporter has difficulty delivering the statement without referring to notes try

– shortening the statement

– doing it in two shots

– using a prompt board behind the camera

– hanging notes below the camera lens with sticky tape.

It's not necessary to have a mike in shot. If you do have one, make sure it isn't big and ugly, especially if your reporter is small and pretty.

Briefing Number Eleven
Walking Interviews and Car Interviews

Interviews with people who are on the move make a pleasant change from the more usual static set-up. They are not particularly difficult to do if conditions are right.

The first requirement is a smooth path or road to walk or drive along. These are needed more for the cameraman than the interviewee. For a walking interview the cameraman has to shoot while going backwards or sideways – not the easiest way to avoid tripping up on bumps and holes (someone should guide him over such hazards). For a car interview he has the difficult task of holding the camera steady despite the movement of the car; if the road is bumpy his task is impossible.

The second requirement is a consistent level of light over the area where the interview will be shot. Patches of dark shadow or very bright sunlight can be a problem as it's not easy for the cameraman to adjust the exposure while on the move.

walking interview shots

Most of a walking interview should be shot in two-shot; a mid-shot or close-up of the interviewee may be difficult to hold steady for long. But don't make the shot too wide, or the sound may be difficult to record. Usually camera and sound walk backwards directly in front of the interviewee and interviewer. Or camera and sound can walk a little to one side of them – and then let them walk past out of shot (remember that they should walk into the next shot from the opposite side of the picture). If the path is very smooth, it may be possible to pull the cameraman backwards on a trolley or in a wheelchair. And if the walk seems to be going on too long, you can always arrange for the interviewee and interviewer to stop at a convenient wall or bench and finish the interview there.

You will need a lot of cutaways to edit a walking interview, especially ones that disguise the fact that your interviewee and interviewer have suddenly jumped down the street as the result of your cuts. Shots of walking feet and listening shots are useful for this. Otherwise shots from behind, shots from the side, and long shots are suitable.

car interviews

For interviews with people driving cars there are usually only three possible camera positions. The cameraman can either sit in the front passenger seat, or he can crouch down on the floor where the front passenger's feet would be. Or he can sit in the back and shoot across the front passenger seat (if the front seats have headrests, make sure they can be removed, or shots from the back won't look good). The driver can usually help the shot by sitting a little bit sideways to favour the camera. Don't forget that the driver should be wearing a seatbelt.

You will have to do separate shots, from the back seat, of the interviewer sitting in the front passenger seat asking questions and listening. Other useful cutaways are shots of the driver's hands (steering, changing gear and so on); shots from the back through the driving mirror (you will have to angle it specially); shots through the side and front windows of the area you are driving through, and shots from the roadside of the car driving past. If the road is smooth, the light is even and the car engine isn't too noisy, you shouldn't have many problems. One advantage with walking and driving interviews is that profile shots for some reason are acceptable. Perhaps it's because the moving background means that the viewer doesn't have just half a face to look at.

SUMMARY BRIEFING NUMBER ELEVEN

Walking Interviews and Car Interviews

Walking Interviews

Shoot walking interviews in two-shot to steady the shot.

For *shots* the cameraman can

– walk backwards directly in front of the interviewee and interviewer

– walk a little to one side, and then let them walk past the camera still talking (remember they enter the next shot from the opposite side)

– be pulled backwards on a trolley or in a wheelchair.

For *cutaways* shoot

– walking feet

– listening shots

– shots from behind

– shots from the side

– long shots

Car Interviews

The cameraman can sit

– in the front passenger seat

– on the floor in front of the front passenger seat

– in the back seat shooting across the front seats (make sure any headrests are removable).

Don't forget the driver should wear a seatbelt.

For *cutaways* shoot

– interviewer listening

– driver's hands

– shots through the driving mirror

– shots of the outside through the car windows

– shots from the roadside of the car passing.

Profile shots are acceptable for interviews on the move.

Briefing Number Twelve
Miming

The other name for miming is shooting to playback, which gives a more complete description of what the technique involves.

The theory is quite simple. If you are not using an existing record or tape, you arrange to make a good quality recording in a sound studio. This recording is known as the master. You then decide on the location and the shots you want for each bit of the song. The sound recordist plays back the relevant bit to the singer through a loudspeaker or an earpiece and the singer sings in time with this playback. This performance is shot and recorded in sync to act as a guide track for the editor. He then edits the pictures so that they are in sync with the master recording. And that's the end of the process.

Of course it's not quite as easy as it sounds (it never is). You have to shoot generous overlaps so that the editor can make the cuts as smooth as possible. You have to be very careful when shooting close-ups of the singer; sound travels so slowly that the singer has to keep a tiny bit ahead of the playback if the timing is to be precisely right and that's a very difficult thing to do.

You can help by placing the loudspeaker as close to the singer as possible, but it must stay out of shot. This can be a problem with long-shots; try and find somewhere to hide it near the singer and hope that the sound recordist has enough cable to reach that far from the recorder.

The difficult thing is trying to find something for the singer to do while he is miming. Wandering round the local park, beach or beauty spot sniffing the flowers has been done before and really isn't original enough.

So go back to the song and think hard what it is about. Can you think of an unusual location which might give it a new slant? Somewhere which would give added meaning to the words? Do the words suggest a prop which might motivate some of the shots? Would it help if you shot the song in several locations? In the middle of a crowd of shoppers? In a factory? On a boat? Next to the airport? In the zoo? Does the singer actually have to mime at all? Could you not shoot him or her just doing something while the song is being played?

Finding settings for slow love songs is particularly difficult and there should come a point while you are trying to think of suitable locations when you ask yourself: why do I want to shoot this song to playback anyway? If you have an orchestra and studio available and can't come up with an original idea, perhaps you should record the song in the studio and rely on songs which bring original locations to mind more readily to provide the breath of fresh air your programme needs.

Miming should be used very sparingly in the studio. The only reason for doing it at all is that there aren't any musicians available at the right time. Pre-recording music so that you don't have so many mikes on the set doesn't seem a very convincing reason when you consider how unobtrusive modern mikes are. If you are worried about the quality of the singer, it's unlikely that he or she will be better miming than in performance. You might get a better sound performance if you have several goes at each number and it's true that there usually is more time for this in a sound only studio. But what you gain in performance you lose in synchronisation. Faking has to be very well done indeed before it is better than the real thing.

SUMMARY BRIEFING NUMBER TWELVE

Miming

This is the procedure for shooting to playback (miming):

1 Record a good quality master in a sound studio (if not using an existing tape or record)

2 Select the location(s)

3 Shoot the singer singing to playback and use this performance as a guide track

4 Editor assembles the shots in sync with the master recording.

Remember to shoot overlaps and place the playback speaker as close to the singer as possible (but out of shot).

Try and find original locations (not the park, beach or local beauty spot every time).

Use miming sparingly in the studio. The real thing is usually better, even for weak artists. What you might gain in performance you usually lose in synchronisation.

Briefing Number Thirteen
Picture Composition

It isn't fair. Some people have a natural feel for composing a picture. There are cameramen who can walk and sway and pan and zoom and all the time what they are shooting sits beautifully in the picture, satisfyingly and perfectly framed. Their pictures seem almost to glow.

The rest of us will have to develop what sense of composition we have by thinking about what makes a good picture and learning to look.

things to avoid

Probably the best way to start is to think about the things not to have in the picture. Chins resting on the bottom of the screen, heads bumping against the top, ears cut off at the side (remember the cut-off strip round the edge of the screen) – these are the obvious things to avoid. Flat-looking pictures with a background object (perhaps a bunch of flowers or a telegraph pole) sprouting from the top of someone's head, strong horizontal lines coming out of either ear – these are ridiculous and should also be avoided. Nor is the back of an interviewer's head and shoulders blocking half the screen in a two-shot particularly attractive.

All these points are really very obvious. But they are things which everyone has seen in programmes because many people in television just don't look at the pictures they produce. They remember what they wanted the picture to say and then let their brain direct their eyes to concentrate on that part only (in the two-shot example I have just mentioned they don't see the head and shoulders blocking the screen because they look only at the interviewee). They don't see the shot as it really is, and as the camera sees it. The camera records everything impartially: its brains must come from the cameraman, the director and the other technicians, who all work together to compose shots which lead the viewers' eyes to the important things on the screen. This is done, of course, by using lighting, sound, camera angles and movements, the position of people and things in the screen, and so on.

learn to look

In order to orchestrate these elements successfully you should first of all devote some time to learning to see things as they really are, as impartially as the camera. Look around you now. Look at the obvious things: I see a sofa, a reading lamp (switched off), bookshelves and two pictures on the wall. The camera would give more emphasis to the lampshade (it's lighter in colour than the rest of the scene), the red plastic toy on the ground (I like to see things tidier than they really are), a blob of blackness where the bookshelves are (they're not lit), and two gold-coloured picture frames (the pictures themselves are too dark and detailed for the camera to record). If I want to take a shot of my sofa, lamp, bookshelves and pictures, I will have to remove the toy (unless I want the viewers to notice it), relight the scene and choose the angle from which I take my shot very carefully.

Once you have had a little practice at seeing pictures the way the camera sees them, it takes less and less conscious effort and eventually becomes second nature. It's rather like the warning marks at the end of each reel of film in the cinema; some people have to have them pointed out to begin with, but after that they spot the marks without any conscious effort at all.

What else can you do to improve the look of your pictures? Common sense and experience are the best guides, but there are some general principles which can help.

A person's face (and most shots in television are of people's faces) sits comfortably in the picture when the bridge of the nose (which is where spectacles rest) is about two-thirds of the way up the picture. If the person is looking to one side, he should be slightly on the other side of the picture – he should be given what is called 'looking room'. If he doesn't have it, he will appear to the viewer to be staring uncomfortably at the side of the screen.

Looking room

In the same way a walking person needs to be given 'walking room'. But you don't have to worry about giving a car

'driving room' because the central point of interest is really the driver of the car and not its bonnet.

Give your pictures depth by making sure that not everyone and everything is in a straight line across the picture. Putting something in the foreground of the picture also gives depth, as does making sure that the lighting isn't the same throughout the picture.

Because the screen is small and therefore tends to be intimate, close-ups have more impact on television than long shots (though an unrelieved diet of close-ups would soon become unwatchable). But don't leave shots looser than they need be – a 'dead' area of picture left unnecessarily round the point of interest in the shot seriously weakens its impact.

No

Yes

Shots taken from normal eye-height tend to be the least interesting because that is what the viewer sees every day. This doesn't mean you have to shoot everything from eye-catching angles, but if you can add something to what the shot is saying by choosing an original angle you should do so.

The most important thing in composition is to decide on the main point of interest in the picture and then frame your shot so that the viewer's eye is led towards it. Your main point can be in the centre of frame, in the foreground or in the background: its relationship to other things in the picture, the camera angle, lighting, and the way the camera moves and things in the picture move all can be used to direct the viewer's eyes where you wish. The thing to avoid is a general shot which leaves the viewer wondering which bit of the picture he is supposed to be looking at and asking himself: 'What exactly is the shot trying to say?'
It's a question you should be constantly asking yourself.

You can cultivate your sense of composition by looking at paintings and photographs. Where has the artist placed the main point of interest in the frame and why? Often a striking picture will place its subject not at all where you would expect it – try and work out how the artist has then balanced his picture to make it a satisfying whole. You can also learn a lot by doing some painting and photography yourself.

The point about most television pictures is of course that they move and are accompanied by sound. To study the way this affects composition you have to watch programmes or go to the cinema. You shouldn't limit yourself to films of your own culture only, any more than you should look at photographs and paintings from your own culture only. Try Indian, Chinese, South American, Indonesian, Middle Eastern, African and Russian films as well. Picture composition varies between cultures and each culture should remain open to foreign influences while developing its own style of television. Just make sure that in the eyes of your own culture it is good television, and good-looking television.

SUMMARY BRIEFING NUMBER THIRTEEN

Picture Composition

Avoid

– chins resting on the bottom of the screen

– heads bumping against the top

– objects sprouting out of people's heads

– horizontal lines coming out of their ears

– the interviewer's back blocking half the screen in two-shots.

Do

– position the bridge of the nose about two-thirds of the way up the screen

– give 'looking room' and 'walking room'

– give pictures depth by having something in the foreground and making sure the lighting isn't too even

– make sure shots are not looser than they need be

– be on the look-out for original angles for shots.

What exactly is the shot trying to say?

Learn to look by studying paintings, photographs, television and films from all cultures.

Briefing Number Fourteen
Graphics

The title and credits in your programme, supers for the names of the people who appear in it, maps, diagrams, graphs, drawings, paintings, animations and slides – graphic design can contribute a huge range of material to your programme, anything from a caption to a computer simulation.

The main rule about graphic design is simple: involve the designer early. Illustrations, paintings, diagrams and in particular animations can take a long time to prepare.

If your programme is likely to have a large graphic content, consult the designer at the treatment stage. Computers have revolutionised graphic techniques and styles and the designer will be able to advise you on what is appropriate, available and – even more important – affordable. Talking to the designer as early as the treatment stage gives your ideas (and the designer's) a chance to develop. You may not be absolutely clear yourself how the completed graphics should look; this doesn't matter as long as you are clear about what it is intended to do. The graphic designer is trained to help you get your message over as long as you can explain what the message is.

The other thing to remember is to collect all your graphics at least twenty-four hours before going into the studio and to check them personally. It must never happen that the first time you see the completed work is when it is on camera in the studio. Mistakes are always cropping up in unexpected places (particularly spelling mistakes) and you must allow time for finding and correcting them. You may also want to make changes (keep these to a minimum). For more complicated areas of graphic design such as animated sequences you will obviously need to view and discuss progress more regularly with the designer.

Titles, Credits and Name Captions
Go and see your designer personally with the exact wording and discuss with him or her the following:

– the size and type of lettering

– capitals or lower case letters?

– the part of the picture the words are intended for ('top third', 'bottom third' or 'centre frame')

– which side the margin should be on: left or right – or do you want straight margins on both sides?

– the colour of the lettering and background (though remember that supers can be coloured electronically in the studio)

– whether the captions will be superimposed on other pictures or have a plain black or coloured background.

titles

Keep all your captions short and simple. With names of ordinary people you don't have to include titles like Mr, Mrs, Miss, Ms or Madam. But Generals, Admirals, Bishops and other elevated people generally like their titles to appear.

dates

With dates you don't need to mention the year if it's the present year. You don't need to write 'st', 'nd', 'rd' and 'th' after the days of the month. Remember also that people usually have to think for a moment before they can tell you what day of the month it is (if they know at all) and so it's helpful to give the day of the week as well:

WEDNESDAY, 19 NOVEMBER

Or if you prefer: WED. 19 NOV.

Or a mixture of the two: WED. 19 NOVEMBER

It's also best to give the name of the month rather than the number. Few people can tell you instantly that 23/7 is in July – almost everyone has to do some mental counting first.

times

When giving times of the day, don't be caught out saying things like

TOMORROW EVENING AT 9PM

9pm is always in the evening. Either pm or EVENING is enough; you don't need to mention both.

Make sure you keep names and captions on the screen long enough for slower readers to take in. A good way to judge how long is to read the caption slowly to yourself two or three times before taking it off.

making letters easy to read

Words can be difficult to read on the screen, particularly if there are a lot of them (when you are subtitling a foreign language film, for example). Black or coloured edging added to the letters electronically in the studio can make them easier to read. If this doesn't work, you may have to ask the vision mixer to black out the portion of the screen behind the words to make them stand out more clearly. It's best always to err on the side of clarity, as many of your viewers

193

will be watching badly tuned sets receiving signals through inadequate aerials.

credits   Try and keep the number of credits to the minimum. Your station probably has a policy written down somewhere which recommends who should and who should not have a credit. Find out what that policy is and stick to it. It's very tedious for viewers to have to sit through a never-ending list which names anyone who ever came near your programme while it was being made.

Maps and Graphs
These should be simple, clear and stripped of all unnecessary information. You should mark on your map the names of all towns, rivers, mountains and so on which you mention in the programme. If you don't mention them, don't mark them.

Graphs must have a title (JAPANESE CAR EXPORTS) and their axes should be labelled clearly (CARS IN THOUSANDS on the vertical axis, YEAR on the horizontal axis). The message of the graph must be simple and immediately obvious or many viewers will miss the point – remember they can't dictate the length of time it is there to be studied, as they can with graphs in newspapers.

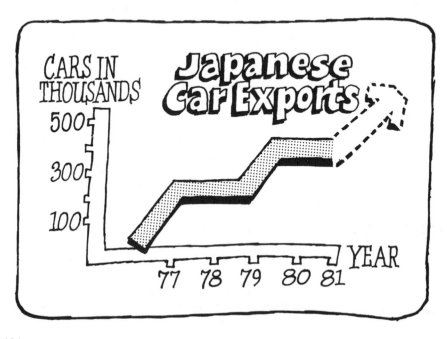

If you can animate graphs in a simple way, so much the better. If you can't animate them (perhaps there isn't time for the graphic designer to do the work), see whether a pan or zoom or cut can help get the message over.

Don't forget that you can superimpose simple maps and graphs over pictures; this can improve their presentation greatly. But clarity must come before presentation. If the pictures get in the way of the message, use the maps and graphs on a plain background.

It's also worth bearing in mind that many people will be watching in black and white; your graphic material must be clear for these viewers as well.

Animations
Elaborate types of animation like cartoon films cost a lot, take months to do and are out of the question for most television programmes. If you really need an animated sequence, don't forget puppets; with CSO and imagination they can be adapted to do most jobs. Simpler animation such as the 'reveal' technique illustrated here is also worth using and doesn't take too long to prepare.

The Reveal Technique

The great thing about animation is that you can use it to steer the viewer around a map or diagram which he might otherwise find difficult to understand. Of course even if you don't have animation in your programme, you should be using camera movements and close-ups on your graphic material to make its message as clear as possible.

Slides

If you are using slides, check that they are clean. Enormous greasy finger and thumb prints are all too easy to miss in the hectic atmosphere of the studio. But they are all too easy to see for the viewer at home.

Press Cuttings

These are always a problem to present attractively. They are rarely the right shape for the television screen and almost always contain more words than you can expect the viewer to want to read. Here is a story showing four methods of dealing with cuttings.

Presenting Newspaper
Cuttings

Presenter:
'Now a cautionary tale for anyone who's thinking of buying a new suit. It could cost more than you expect.'

Voice:
'Ill-fitting suits wreck wedding and put groom in court.
The long and short of bridegroom James Moore's ill-fitting wedding suit cost him his bride – and a fifty pound fine yesterday.'

Presenter:
'That's a lot to pay – and it doesn't even include the cost of the suits. The first one bought by the unfortunate Mr Moore was too small. So he dashed out and bought another – only to find it was too big. Teasingly he told his bride-to-be:'

Voice:
'I'm not wearing this down the aisle. It's all off.'

196

Presenter:
'His bride, Miss Caroline Mortimer, believed him. So the next day Moore and his relations waited over an hour for her to show up at the church.'

Voice:
'Moore then raced round to Miss Mortimer's house only to be told that his bride wanted nothing more to do with him. In a fit of anger Moore then kicked out all the lights on Miss Mortimer's car and ripped both wing mirrors off causing over a hundred and thirty pounds damage.'

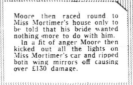

Moore then raced round to Miss Mortimer's house only to be told that his bride wanted nothing more to do with him.
In a fit of anger Moore then kicked out all the lights on Miss Mortimer's car and ripped both wing mirrors off causing over £130 damage.

METHOD 3
PLACE CUTTING ON A BACKGROUND WHICH MAKES IT LOOK GOOD

Presenter:
'That lot landed him in court and cost him the fifty pound fine.
A last word from the would-be groom':

Voice:
'I have lost two stone with the worry and embarrassment since it all began. I think I will remain a bachelor for ever.'

' I have lost two stone with the worry and embarrassment since it all began. I think I will remain a bachelor for ever '

METHOD 4
ASK GRAPHICS TO PUT YOUR QUOTES ON CAPTIONS

Presenter:
'Suit yourself, Mr Moore. But I doubt you'll save much money that way. After all the weight you've lost, your old suits must be a bit loose. Anyone know a good tailor?'

Of course it would be unusual to use all four methods in the same story. Find which style suits your story best and stick to it. Once again don't forget you can do a lot to enliven press cuttings by using camera movements and zooms. The extra voice to read the cuttings is also important: the impact of the story is lessened if the presenter reads the extracts as well. And the voice must read the words on the screen accurately: missing out a phrase or reading words which aren't there looks and sounds careless.

Photographs and Drawings
It helps if these fit the proportions of the television screen (4 units across by 3 units down) but obviously if they don't, you will have to frame them on camera as best you can. Photographs should be matt finish (not glossy) to avoid reflections from the lights. They should be mounted on stiff card by the graphic designer so that they lie flat – creased and wrinkled illustrations look awful and should never be allowed on to the screen.

You can successfully produce whole sequences or even programmes using just photographs or drawings. Think of camera movements and close-ups to bring out the important details in the pictures. If the drawings are specially made for your programme, ask the graphic designer if some of them could be animated using the 'reveal' technique. Still sequences can be very effective cut to music; they can be even more effective if accompanied by well-chosen sound effects.

Some situations are actually easier to cover using stills only. Suppose you want to show a child being taken out to see the Christmas decorations at night in a big city. A sequence like this can be expensive and difficult to shoot on video or film: lighting problems, overtime for the camera crew and the limit on the number of hours you can reasonably keep a seven-year-old out of bed could make this a tricky assignment. If you use stills, however, you have at your disposal very high-speed films and flash: a good stills photographer can take dozens of photographs in different locations in a fraction of the time a video or film cameraman would need.

You can record the child's reactions and the sounds of the Christmas crowds at night on a tape recorder. When the stills have been developed you pick the best ones and tape or film them, perhaps introducing a few camera movements. You then edit the shots and sound track in the normal way (without any sync problems to worry about) and with luck and the addition of some carefully chosen Christmas music you should end up with a very nice sequence.

rostrum camera

It is possible to put your stills on videotape or film using a normal studio or location camera. But for really smooth and accurate camera movements and anything that's more complicated than a zoom it's best to have the stills shot on a special rig known as a rostrum camera which is designed to give maximum control of camera movements over small areas.

Preparing a photograph for rostrum camera

It's not usually necessary to be present when your stills are being shot by the rostrum cameraman. But you do have to give him exact instructions about what you want. The best way to do this is to fix a sheet of tracing paper over each still

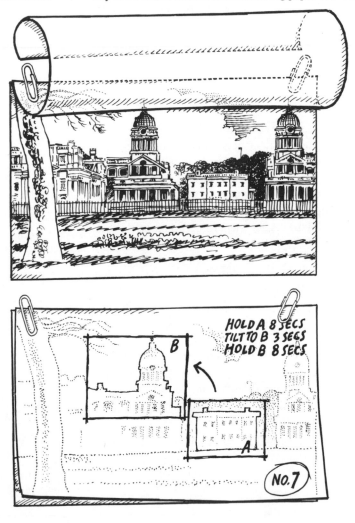

A simple way of getting correct TV proportions. Place angle A in bottom left-hand corner of desired frame. Any line from the slope to the base will give you the correct height-to-base proportion.

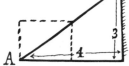

with paperclips, number the still and trace the outline of some easily recognisable feature in the still so that the rostrum cameraman can realign the paper correctly if it moves. Then take another piece of greaseproof paper and make a large right-angled triangle (as shown in the illustration) to check that the shots you mark up are the right proportions for the screen. Letter the opening and closing frames of each shot and specify the speed of the movements by 'seeing' the movement on your mental TV and counting how many seconds it takes. Don't forget to ask the cameraman to hold each shot steady for about 8 seconds before and after each movement – here's another chance to get three shots for the price of one.

SUMMARY BRIEFING NUMBER FOURTEEN

Graphics

Two general points:

– involve the designer early

– collect graphics early to allow time for alterations and corrections. Check all graphics personally.

Titles, Credits and Name Captions

Write out the exact wording you want and discuss the following with the designer: lettering, capitals/lower case, position in picture, margin, colour, background.

Keep all captions short and simple.

Mention VIP titles only.

People rarely know the day of the month or recognise the number of the month instantly. So name the day of the week and the month – use short versions if you want.

Cut out excess information – 'tomorrow evening at 9 pm'.

Keep captions on the screen long enough for slower readers (read each one to yourself slowly 2 or 3 times).

For legibility use black or coloured edging. Or wipe in a plain background from the studio.

Keep the number of credits to the minimum.

Maps and Graphs

Don't include unnecessary information

Give graphs a title and label the axes clearly. Animation or camera movements or cuts can help get your message across.

Superimposing simple maps or graphs over a picture can make them look good, but don't sacrifice clarity.

Don't forget that viewers of black and white sets also like to know what is going on.

Animations

Cartoons are usually too expensive – try puppets instead.

Simpler animation such as the 'reveal' technique is well worth using.

Slides

Make sure they are clean.

Press Cuttings

Difficult to show attractively. Try

– using extracts that fit the screen (as well as the story)

– masking unwanted words

– placing the cutting on a good-looking background

– putting your quotes on captions.

Also use camera movements and zooms. And an extra voice to read out the words exactly as shown on screen.

Photographs and Drawings

Mount them on stiff card. Photos should be matt if possible.

Still sequences are cheap, relatively easy to do and can be very effective if used with sound effects or music.

For rostrum camera shots

– cover each still with greaseproof paper

– number each still

– mark up shots using triangle guide

– specify timings

– ask for holds before and after camera movements (three shots for the price of one).

Briefing Number Fifteen
Whose Programme is it?

It takes a lot of people to make a television programme: technicians, contributors, bosses and of course you the producer. Some of these people may get very involved with the programme, almost as involved as you. The cameraman, the editor, the presenter, the major contributor and your boss may even start to refer to the programme as 'my' programme. Don't worry about this, as it's usually a good sign. Everybody likes to be involved with a winner; they shun a loser.

But what happens when you have an argument about the programme, or something in it? Whose programme is it then? Who has the final say?

It all depends with whom you are arguing. The first point to be absolutely clear about is that the programme is *yours*. You the producer are the only person who is involved with it from the day it begins to the day it is transmitted, and beyond; you are the person who will get all the blame if things go wrong (if things go right, there will be no shortage of volunteers to take the praise for 'my' programme).

So the programme is first and foremost yours. But this doesn't mean that you should be a petty dictator when dealing with the people who help you make it. Because television is teamwork; you can't do it all yourself.

So with technical matters you would be foolish to disregard the advice of the cameraman, sound man or editor; they almost certainly have more experience to draw on than you. If you are having a dispute with a contributor you probably know more about what's right for television than he does; listen to him, by all means, but never allow the editorial control to slip from your hands. But all the members of the team (except for you) are experts only so far as their part of the programme is concerned. So the final decision in any disagreement with them is yours, because only you know how each part of the programme fits.

Disputes with your boss are more tricky to resolve. In the first place you should prevent most of them arising by telling him at each stage of the production what you are up to, so that when he comes to see the edited programme or watch you recording in the studio, there won't be any surprises for him. If he does want to make some changes which you don't agree with, you are of course entitled to try and persuade him to do it your way. But in the end you will probably have to give way, because he is the boss.

Giving way is not necessarily a bad thing – don't underestimate the contribution a good boss can make. He knows the background to the programme and can also approach it with a fresh eye at a time when you may be so hopelessly caught up in the details that you find it impossible to stand back and assess the impact of the programme as a whole.

SUMMARY BRIEFING NUMBER FIFTEEN

Whose Programme is it?

Other people may call the programme 'my' programme but it belongs to you the producer more than anyone. You are the only one who stays with the programme right through the production process.

If you can't agree about something with

– a cameraman, sound man, editor or other technician: listen to their advice, but the final decision is yours.

– a contributor: again listen, but the final decision is yours.

– your boss: you will probably have to give way. Minimise the chances of disagreement by keeping him informed at all stages of the production. Bear in mind his criticism may be valid as he comes fresh to the programme.

Briefing Number Sixteen
Style in Commentary Writing

Words are first-class for communicating with people if used well. If used badly or there are too many of them they just get in the way.

So you have to make every word in a commentary count. Think of this while you are writing it. Then when you have finished writing, go through crossing out all the words and phrases which contribute little to the meaning. Then read the commentary out loud and you'll spot more words and phrases which won't be missed. When you have crossed those out, you will be left with a commentary which (with luck) gets your message across simply, clearly and briefly.

drop the meaningless

How do you recognise the words and phrases to drop? The key to this is always the meaning. Many phrases don't mean anything, phrases like *let's face it, if you ask me, you have to admit, when all is said and done.* They are expressions which people use to keep talking while they are thinking of what to say next and should have no place in your commentary. Sometimes these phrases can be as long as sentences: *it is also of importance to bear in mind the following considerations . . ..* But they still don't mean anything, except perhaps *listen*, which you don't need to say anyway.

Many individual words are also meaningless: *well* at the beginning of a sentence; *interpersonal* in the phrase interpersonal relationships (how else do people have relationships?); *profoundly* in the sentence: *he was profoundly impressed by her ability.* Surely the simpler *he was impressed by her ability* is more powerful?

Give your commentaries clarity and impact by also dropping all those words which weaken their neighbours, words like *quite, almost, perhaps, about.* If you are sure of your facts, pick the appropriate word and let it stand without qualification.

You can go through your script and weed out almost all the adjectives without losing any meaning. If the object or person you are describing is in the picture, adjectives are unlikely to add much. For example – *Ali Smith, a good-looking young bus conductor, found the bomb.* Far better to say, *Ali Smith, a bus conductor, found the bomb.* This leaves you room to add something about how, when or where Ali Smith found the bomb – or even tell viewers how old he is.

don't state the obvious	Check that you aren't stating the obvious in your commentary. Some examples: *this tropical island set in the sunny blue sea will make an ideal holiday spot* (where else but in the sea would you find an island?); *at the end of the week he picked up his wages for the work he had done* (what else are wages paid for?); *there are many sick people in the hospital* (it would be surprising if there were not).
avoid jargon	Another thing to avoid is jargon. After researching a programme on airlines you yourself are probably familiar with airways jargon like ATC, passenger seat miles, short-haul destinations, and so on. But don't expect your viewers to be. Jargon is a shorthand language for specialists; if you want to give your commentary an authentic flavour, by all means use one or two jargon expressions but make sure they are explained in everyday language.
initials	You should never introduce sets of initials without explaining them in full at least once (ATC stands for Air Traffic Control). But viewers probably won't remember their meaning for long, especially if you have introduced other sets of unfamiliar initials like CAT (Clear Air Turbulence) and VMC (Visual Meteorological Conditions).
clichés	Clichés are another thing to be wary of. In some ways clichés are comfortable and reassuring because they are familiar. Expressions like *to all intents and purposes, this day and age, at this point in time, ill-luck* which always *dogs* people, determination which is always *ruthless* – expressions like these communicate meaning to the viewer in a flash. But is it the precise meaning which you want to communicate? Often the comfortable cliché which presents itself so quickly is only roughly right for what you want to say. A moment's thought would uncover a better arrangement of words which would express your meaning more precisely and more economically.
brevity is better	When you are writing commentary, keep your sentences short. If they are more than two or three lines long, you are probably trying to get too many thoughts into too short a space and the viewer may not follow your argument. The same goes for words: short words are better than long words because people understand them more easily. So *start* is better than *initiate, show* is better than *manifest, weather* is better than *meteorological* and *end* is better than *terminate*.

Remember the viewer hears a commentary; he can't read it. Moreover he hears it only once and not at a pace of his own choosing. So its meaning must be instantly clear. You can cash in on the fact that the viewer will have the commentary read to him by letting the inflection of the commentator's voice get some of the meaning across. So you will often find that replacing *which* and *that* with a dash works well.

For example the sentence

the People's Stadium, which was the scene of his greatest triumphs, was renamed in his honour

is easier to read and has more impact when written thus:

the People's Stadium – the scene of his greatest triumphs – was renamed in his honour.

If you find it difficult to put your thoughts down on paper clearly and simply, use the trick of telling someone aloud what you want to say. Your brain will throw out most of the padding automatically. People talk more clearly than they write; so make your writing more like your talking and your viewers will understand you better.

Note:
Readers who would like to learn more about good writing are recommended to study *The Complete Plain Words* by Sir Ernest Gowers published by Penguin Books.

Good writing is not just an extra refinement to round off your other abilities. It's more important than that, because in many ways your words *are* your thoughts. If your thoughts aren't clear, it will show up in your words.

SUMMARY BRIEFING NUMBER SIXTEEN

Style in Commentary Writing

Make every word in a commentary count.

Always think of the meaning of what you are saying.

Drop meaningless words, phrases, sentences

– words which weaken their neighbours

– unnecessary adjectives

– phrases and sentences which state the obvious

– jargon and clichés.

Always tell the viewer what sets of initials stand for.

Don't use too many initials in your programme.

Use short words and short sentences.

Replace *which* and *that* with a dash where appropriate.

Make your writing as clear as your talking.

Your words are your thoughts. If your thoughts are clear, your words will be.

Briefing Number Seventeen
Legal Problems

This Briefing is not a guide for producers on how to stay out of trouble with the law; that would be impossible for any one book to provide because legal and broadcasting practices differ widely around the world. The only practical advice I can offer is that you should find out who is the lawyer in your station and refer to him whenever you think you are going to have problems; often a tiny change of procedure (sometimes even a tiny change of wording) will save you endless trouble later.

Which are the areas most likely to bring you into contact with the law?

shooting permission
The most common pitfall is getting permission to shoot on location. Obviously you have to have permission to shoot inside a home or factory, but do you need permission to shoot outside? In most countries you may shoot the outside of private property without permission as long as your camera is on a public right of way. But do you need police permission to shoot on the public highway? In some countries you do.

paying artistes
Does your station normally pay contributors to programmes? If so, how much? You obviously have to pay presenters, artistes, actors, singers and so on, but does the fee cover rehearsals and repeats? And what about video cassette sales? Who fixes the fees and sends out the contracts? What about interviewees in current affairs and documentary programmes – are they paid? These questions are not only significant for your budget, but they also have a bearing on the amount of interference you might have to accept from a contributor. As a general rule editorial control should stay with you as the representative of the TV station, but what happens if someone agrees to give you an interview only on condition that he can see the edited interview before it is transmitted? Do you the producer have the authority to agree to such a demand? It's best to check beforehand what to do.

copyright
Copyright is another area you should find out about. Generally speaking, if you use someone else's play, short story, film, photograph, or music you have to pay for the privilege. But your station may have a special deal with the organisations which protect copyright and the policy may be to use only those items covered by the deal and never touch

the rest. Obviously it's worth knowing what the arrangements are.

libel
Libel is probably the most serious legal mess you can get yourself into. The dangers, definitions and defences for libel are complicated, but don't be put off finding out what the practice in your country is; you'll probably find it a fascinating subject. And you may be surprised to discover that in your country as in Britain truth is only a complete defence to a libel action if you can prove it. It's no use just knowing that you are right . . .

SUMMARY BRIEFING NUMBER SEVENTEEN

Legal Problems

Practical advice: find out who your station's lawyer is and refer suspected difficulties to him *before* they get serious.

Areas in which you need to know your local law:

– location shooting permission

– artist's contracts

– editorial control

– copyright

– libel.

Briefing Number Eighteen
Who are the Viewers?

Is there anyone out there?

It's not a question which producers ask themselves every day. The answer leads to other questions, which in time lead into the area of broadcasting policy, over which producers have little control. Anyway, you may say, you are much too busy finishing your programme to think about such problems. You may even believe that whether the programme attracts one viewer or a million doesn't make much difference to the process of making it . . .

But it ought to. It's important every now and then to step back and ask yourself (as your bosses should constantly be doing): Whom am I broadcasting to? The young? The old? Graduates or non-graduates? Government officials, academics and managers? Or workers and their families?

The answer to this question affects a lot of things in your programme. It affects the subjects you choose: the young don't have the same things on their minds as the old, VIPs have different problems from workers. It affects the language you use over the air: the educated don't always speak the same language as the uneducated and the two don't necessarily understand each other. It affects the sort of people who appear in your programme: should they be mainly officials – or ordinary people? It affects the type of music you broadcast: should it be traditional or imported, classical or pop? It affects the sort of sport, dancing and drama you show, the sort of programmes you import . . . when you start thinking about it, it affects virtually everything.

Of course when you do start asking yourself 'Whom am I broadcasting to?', the answer is obvious. For general programmes the majority of viewers will be young or middle-aged, and not so well educated rather than well educated, simply because the majority of most populations is young or middle-aged and not so well educated. Some of the programmes may be designed to appeal to particular groups of people (women, children, sportsmen, the handicapped) but the audience for your general programmes will be made up of the vast mass of ordinary people.

So it seems silly to waste the potential of the most successful medium for mass communication which has ever been devised by doing programmes on subjects which wouldn't even fill a university lecture hall – subjects like the velocity of money or motivations for work, which even academics and executives find difficult to turn their minds to. By all means tackle these subjects occasionally on television, but do so only occasionally, and then in ways which a sizeable chunk of your audience finds interesting. The rest of the time broadcast programmes which interest ordinary people. These are programmes about people – their life, their loves, their work, their successes, their failures, their adventures, their hates, their pleasures, their children, their pets – and programmes with people – singing, dancing, telling jokes, playing sport, cooking, taking part in competitions. People are mainly interested in people.

'Ah, yes, but our station is run by the government and they like us to spend most of our time talking about problems of national importance,' you may say. That may be so, but it's up to you (and the broadcasting authorities) to see that the programmes of national importance don't crowd out the programmes which have popular appeal. Because when the members of the government realise that hardly anyone is watching the programmes of national importance, they will criticise the broadcasters for not doing a good job and they will be right. Though to be fair they should accept part of the blame themselves.

How does all this affect you as a humble producer? There are two lessons which you can take away with you:

1   Choose subjects for programmes which interest you, not subjects you are paid to be interested in.

2   Remember who your viewers are and make your programmes appeal to as wide a section of them as possible.

TV is a *mass* communication medium.

SUMMARY BRIEFING NUMBER EIGHTEEN

Who are the Viewers?

Young or old? Graduates or non-graduates? VIPs or workers? The answers affect

– the subjects you choose

– the language you use

– the sort of people who appear on TV

– the music you choose

– the sorts of programme you broadcast.

People like programmes about people.

Governments like popular, successful TV stations. So choose subjects which interest you and make your programmes appeal to as wide a section of the public as possible.

TV is a *mass* communication medium.

Briefing Number Nineteen
Working with Actors

Actors present a challenge different from any other you will meet in programme-making. On the one hand actors are human beings: this means that they have their own ideas and experience to bring to the programme. On the other hand – unlike participants in most other programmes – they are almost completely under the control of the producer. Words, gestures, movements, costume, make-up – everything about actors comes under your direction. The trick is to exercise your control without suffocating their initiative.

studying the script

You have to be extremely well prepared if you are to do this successfully. The first place you should turn to for inspiration is the script, which we will assume has been written by someone else and has to be followed faithfully (your job is first to try and make the script work as it stands; if later during rehearsals you find it doesn't work, that is the time to suggest or make changes). When you first look through the script you should read it only for pleasure. Only then when you have enjoyed the script yourself, should you start working to let the viewer share your enjoyment.

Start by working through the script again two or three times in great detail, thinking about the most effective way for each character to look, sound and move, and considering the most effective way for each line to be spoken. It is not necessary at this stage to make final decisions about each point. A careful review of the possibilities is all that is needed. You must leave room for the actors to make their creative contributions.

casting

This preliminary study of the script on your own will be a great help when you come to casting the actors. If you have a large number of actors to choose from and the budget for your production is large enough, it's worth employing a casting director to help you. He or she will know better than you which actors are available and what they can do. This specialist knowledge can save you a lot of time and also improve your chances of getting the right actor for each part. Good casting is vital to the success of your play; you should take a great deal of trouble over it. If you get it right, half your problems are over. If you get it badly wrong, you will have to work flat out just to avoid a disaster.

auditioning

You should hold an audition open to anyone who wants to

come – never turn down the chance of finding new talent. Give each candidate a scene or speech to perform and see what they make of it. Don't trust your memory, but make a note about each actor as you go along: how well they perform and how well they suit the part physically. Looks are important, but in the long run being able to put the part over effectively is more important than just looking right.

rehearsals

Once you have chosen your actors, tell them which part they are to play and give them each a copy of the script to study for a few days. You should then arrange to meet for rehearsals. At first these can be in any convenient and quiet place and should be nothing more than a read-through of the script with each actor doing his own part and you listening. An actor's idea of his character in the script may differ from your own, but you should listen to his interpretation carefully, as it may well bring out aspects of the character which you have missed. This is the fascination of working with actors: by talking, experimenting and sweating it out together you should be able to arrive at a performance which is considerably better than any of you could have achieved by yourself. Putting on drama is team work – but don't forget that you are the captain of the team. It's difficult to lay down precise guide-lines how to get the best out of your team – every leader has his own method. The main thing is that you should let everyone contribute what they can and then mould these contributions to fit in with your interpretation of the play as a whole.

working out movements and shots

As rehearsals proceed you should start thinking about what the actors will be doing where, and the shots you will take to cover them. If you are doing your programme away from the studio, you should have chosen the locations; if you are recording in the studio, you should have a floor plan showing the layout of your set. So whether you are using video or film you should already have a good idea of the setting for each scene. Now use your mental TV to imagine your actors in each setting, where they will stand, sit, walk, kneel, or lie down. Then think about where you will place your camera or cameras to cover the story. Think about the most important person, action or thing in each bit of the script and how you can best emphasise that importance with your camera.

rehearsing movements

Once you have worked out positions and movements, start introducing them into your rehearsals. You don't need the full set to do this. Chairs, tables, books, chalk marks on the floor – any of these will do to mark the positions of the props and scenery on the actual set. The size and layout of your makeshift set should be as close to the real thing as possible.

In rehearsals from now on the actors should practise all their moves as well as their words. This will let them get the 'feel' of the area they will be performing in and also gives you the chance of viewing the action from the positions you have planned for your camera. You may well discover better positions and movements for both actors and camera.

long static scenes

Try and avoid long stretches of dialogue during which the actors don't move; very static scenes are difficult to make interesting on the screen. But if you have a long stretch of dialogue don't give up and just cover everything in one general shot. Even if people are only sitting and talking, their relationship changes at each stage of the conversation. When chatting off-camera this change is revealed in the way they interact: leaning forwards or backwards, looking at or away from each other, coughing or just settling into a more comfortable position. You should aim to reproduce this sort of subtle detail in front of the camera. So if your actors are tense and aren't interacting naturally, you must demonstrate what you want by acting through the passage yourself. Then when the actor has got the idea you can use these small but revealing signs of a changing relationship to make decisions about which actor to show on the screen at each point. If you get your cuts right, your viewers will unconsciously absorb this interaction or 'body language' and see the characters in the play as real people going through a real experience which the viewers can share. And even your long static scenes will be worth viewing.

motivate movements

Understanding body language also helps you to motivate your actors' moves. This motivation is important: without it gestures and movements round the set tend to confuse rather than illuminate what the play is trying to say. So give your actor a reason to walk across the room (perhaps he's playing a meticulous character and wants to straighten a picture hanging on the wall). Give your actress a reason for leaning back in her chair (she is getting bored with the conversation). If there is no reason for this sort of movement your viewers will be wondering 'Why is she doing that?' instead of watching the play. The motive for an action needn't be obvious the moment the action begins, but it should emerge sooner or later as the drama develops.

don't allow overacting

One other point about acting. Don't let your actors overact. The television audience is made up of many units of one or two people watching at home and so your actors should perform as if they were playing to one or two viewers sitting no more than a couple of metres away, not an audience of tens of thousands. TV drama is the art of the raised eyebrow, not the grand gesture. Your actors don't have to 'project' their emotions as stage actors have to; they should just behave in character as naturally as possible and let the camera take the message to the audience.

shot sizes

Most of your drama (perhaps as much as two-thirds) can be shot in mid-shots or close-ups, but you will also need two-shots or the occasional long shot to show where people are in relation to each other.

positions in the screen

The position in the screen of each actor in these wide shots is important, as some parts of the screen are stronger than others. For example, a person giving an order should be in a dominating position (in the centre of the screen or in the foreground) and a person receiving an order in a weaker position (at the side or in the background).

There are no hard-and-fast rules about the strong and weak parts of the screen, as the values of the different parts change as the position of the camera changes or the distance between the people in the picture changes. It's enough for you to be aware that these relationships exist and that you can use them to give your drama impact.

'clever-clever' shots

Try and avoid very tricky shots (for example an action covered only by showing its reflection in a glass bottle) unless they really help the story along. Too often 'clever-clever' shots draw attention only to themselves and don't do much for the play as a whole. As a general principle you should aim for a succession of smoothly flowing, well-lit shots (lighting is particularly important in drama) which show the play off to its best advantage rather than dazzle the viewers with their brilliance.

studio productions

When you have finally decided on all your shots, put them into the script and then have the script typed out in the usual way. The procedure for doing a drama in the studio is the same as for any other studio programme (see Chapter Eleven) – you still need to do your shot-by-shot run-through even though you may have been rehearsing with the actors for weeks before. Things always look different in the studio and the technicians also need to rehearse their roles.

For studio productions it's sensible to record the play in large chunks with as few stops as possible and following the order in which it was written. This gives the actors a chance of really getting into their parts and forgetting the television technology all round them. If anything goes wrong, carry on to the end of each section and then go back and repeat the bits which went wrong so that you can edit in the correct version later.

drama on location   For single camera location shooting you will have to break the whole play down into individual shots and light and shoot each one separately. You can save time by shooting all the scenes in one area one after another, just altering the lighting a little. But don't do this if it confuses the actors because you are jumping about the story too much. They are the people your viewers will see and so their needs must be given top priority.

SUMMARY BRIEFING NUMBER NINETEEN

Working with Actors

Start with the script. Read through it first for pleasure. Then work through in detail, thinking about the best way for each character to look, move and say his lines.

Take great care choosing actors. Finding the right person for the part is half the battle. Hold an audition open to all. Remember when casting that being able to act is more important than just looking right.

At rehearsals first listen to the ideas the actors bring to their parts. Then work together with them to mould their roles to fit with your interpretation of the play as a whole. Drama production is team work – with you the captain of the team.

Start thinking about your actors' movements and camera positions. Learn to understand how people 'talk' with their bodies. Introduce these often subtle movements into the play, if the actors aren't already doing them naturally. Motivate all moves: if you don't they will be distracting rather than illuminating.

Practise moves as well as words at rehearsals, using a makeshift set and props to show the dimensions of the real set.

Don't allow overacting. TV drama is the art of the raised eyebrow.

Use mainly mid-shots and close-ups, with occasional long shots to show relationships between actors. Think about strong and weak positions in the screen and shoot actors accordingly.

Avoid 'clever-clever' shots. Take trouble with lighting.

With studio productions follow normal studio procedure, including the shot-by-shot run-through. Shoot the play in order with as few breaks as possible. Reshoot to cover mistakes and edit in correct versions later.

On location light and shoot each shot separately. Don't jump about the script to save time on lighting if it confuses the actors too much.

Give your actors' needs top priority. They are the people the viewers will see.

Briefing Number Twenty
You want to work in Television?

If you are reading this book as part of a student course or because you are thinking of a career in television, you will welcome a few hints about finding a job as a producer.

There are always large numbers of people wanting to join television and so you must try and make yourself stand out from the crowd. The first requirement therefore is probably a college degree; the subject of the degree doesn't matter though obviously if it is a subject you are genuinely interested in, your grade will be better and that won't harm your prospects. But don't feel that you must have a degree in mass communications or media studies to enter television; treat these subjects as worth studying in their own right, not as the back door to a job. Frankly, very little of what you learn as a student of mass communications or anything else will be of direct use to you as a producer. The value of a degree is that it shows that you can study something deeply and know how to think.

There are of course other ways of demonstrating these abilities and so you shouldn't despair if you can't go to college. But non-graduates do find it harder to get an interview and many stations will refuse even to consider them for production jobs (which is unfair, but unfortunately true). If you are in this unhappy position, find out what non-production jobs you would be considered for and apply for those. It may be possible to transfer to production later.

But even a college degree won't guarantee you a job as a producer. To stand out from the crowd of eager graduates you must show that you have done something worthwhile in a field that is relevant or vaguely relevant to television. Obviously to be able to say that you have made (or helped to make) a short video or film programme makes you stand out head and shoulders above everyone else – it doesn't matter if you used professional or amateur equipment, the important thing is to have done it. Producing or directing a play (amateur or professional), an exhibition of your photographs, writing a script, organising a fete or festival or any other evidence of creative or organising ability, will give you a head start. A background in student or professional journalism or radio will also make you stand out.

Having lots of programme ideas will not give you as great an advantage as you might expect. Whatever viewers may think, TV stations on the whole are not short of ideas – they are short of money, air time and perhaps the energy to introduce new ideas. So presenting your own list of ideas is unlikely to excite anyone who might hire you; he is more interested in evidence of your potential ability to turn ideas into programmes. By all means work out a list of good ideas but keep it for the interview, not for your letter of application.

Whatever method you use to show your potential, it has to be backed up by knowing something about television. To do this you have to watch it intensively, putting yourself into the producer's shoes and working out where he has been successful and where he has failed and how you could do it better. Get to know the names of the producers and the programmes they have done; also read the television critics regularly and try and assess the strengths and weaknesses of their criticisms. The object of all this is to be so well briefed that when you go for an interview you are as well informed as anyone already in television. Not a know-all, but pleasantly knowledgeable. It's impressive (and flattering) for anyone in television to meet someone who has paid the medium the compliment of studying it intelligently and sympathetically. You'll find you have lots to talk about at the interview, which will be a refreshing change for your interviewer, who usually spends his time having to ask questions like 'Why do you want to get into television?' Incidentally, one way to answer that question is to say: 'You saw that programme two nights ago about . . . (pick a well-made programme about something you are interested in) – well, that's the sort of programme I would like to make. Though perhaps the programme should have gone into another aspect of the question, namely . . .' How can they resist you?

The obvious person to whom to apply for a job is the Appointments or Personnel Officer; telephone the station to find the exact name and title of the person you should write to. Send details of your age, education, prizes, achievements, interests and so on, paying special attention to those features which make you stand out from the crowd. You don't have to wait for the job to be advertised before you write: television stations often need extra people in a hurry and there is no reason why you shouldn't benefit from this unscheduled recruitment. If you are offered this sort of job, it may be for only a few months or weeks but accept it anyway, because it represents your first foot in the door. The job probably won't be called a producer's job but will have some other title such as assistant producer, trainee producer, research assistant or production assistant. I have called it a producer's job or a production job because television stations use such a wide range of titles for their entry grade.

Don't write just to Appointments or Personnel Officers; try writing also to Heads of Departments, Executive and Senior Producers, or even Producers to ask for work. They are the ones who actually need you to lighten their load and if they suggest to Appointments or Personnel that they would like to try you, they are unlikely to be contradicted.

If you are turned down at first, keep trying. If you are leaving college, haven't yet managed to land a production job in television and have to earn a living while you are trying, journalism and radio are the best havens. Be very careful about accepting a non-production job in television if you have the formal entry requirements (like a degree) and are really determined to become a producer. There is nothing wrong with non-production jobs. But if being a producer is what you are determined to become, starting in a job like secretary or floor manager can put you back a long time, as everyone gets into the habit of thinking of you as a secretary or floor manager. And how many of the existing secretaries and floor managers are already in the queue for transfer to production?

SUMMARY BRIEFING NUMBER TWENTY

You want to work in Television?

Get a college degree – the subject doesn't matter.

If you can't go to college and your TV station considers only graduates for production jobs, apply for any job you can get. It may be possible to transfer later.

Make yourself stand out from the crowd of applicants by

– making (or helping to make) a short film or videotape

– producing or directing a play

– organising an exhibition of your photographs

– writing a script

– organising a fête or festival

– showing evidence of creative or organising ability

– working in student or professional journalism or radio.

Keep a list of programme ideas for the interview.

Back up your achievements by

- watching TV intelligently and sympathetically (think of the producer's problems)
- noting producers' names and programmes
- reading television reviews (you don't have to agree with them).

Telephone to find out the correct name and title of the person to apply to, and send him or her details of personal background, education and achievements.

You don't have to wait for jobs to be advertised before writing; unscheduled recruitment is common and gives you an invaluable foot in the door.

Note that the titles for entry grades into production jobs differ widely.

It's worth writing direct to Heads of Departments, Executive and Senior Producers and Producers as well as the Appointments Department.

Keep trying.

If you have the formal entry requirements for a production job, think twice before accepting a non-production job.

Glossary

Amplitude the strength of an electrical current or voltage (signal)

animation simulating movement by shooting slowly changing position of subject one frame at a time

answer print first fully graded colour print made from cut negative

aperture the opening through which light enters the camera (*see* f-number)

assemble editing making up video programme in correct order on blank tape without prerecorded control track

audio another word for sound; used in contrast to *video*

audition hearing actors to assess suitability for parts in a play

Back light light from behind to separate interviewee from background

big close-up (BCU) very close shot of the face cutting off top of the head. Also shot showing detail of an object

black edging outlining letters on screen to help legibility

buffer shot diguise for crossing the line

Camera card personalised script for studio cameraman

camera left & right left and right from camera position

camera original master copy of reversal film

camera script script which includes full details of shots, lighting, sound, etc.

camera tube device for turning light variations in a scene into electrical variations or signals

caption graphics on a slide or card

carrier regular electrical wave modulated to transmit information

cassette container for magnetic tape (audio or video) which is laced up automatically by recording/playback machine

casting matching actors with roles

chromakey replacing part of an electronic picture with material from another source

chrominance signal portion of the video signal containing colour information made up of colour difference signals

clapper board board used to mark point for synchronising sound and vision and to identify roll, shot and take by numbers

clock (studio) specially designed clock recorded before start of studio recording to act as tape identification and leader

close-up (CU) shot showing person's whole head from collar upwards. Close shot of an object

colour balance ensures camera is combining the three primary colours in correct proportions

colour difference encoding colour information by expressing red and blue signals as value remaining after subtracting luminance signal

colour reversal intermediate (CRI) intermediate film stock for making one or more copies from reversal master

colour separation overlay (CSO) *see* chromakey

commag combined magnetic film – sound is recorded on magnetic stripe running next to the picture

commentary narration added to programme, usually ad lib for sports

computer editing computer lines up video machines and edits as instructed

contrast brightness difference in picture or scene

control track (video) electronic sprocket holes

crab sideways movement of camera

credits list of people involved in making a programme

crossing the line reversing flow of action in successive shots thus confusing viewer's sense of direction

cutaway shot used to avoid a jump cut, usually of something related to, but not seen in, main shot

cue signal for action; *also* continuous passage in a commentary

cue dot electronic marker points on videotape

cycle (electrical) one complete repetition of alternating current or voltage, described by frequency in units called Hertz. UK mains operate on 50 cycles a second (50 Hz), US on 60 (60 Hz)

cyclorama (cyc) curtain providing blank general background in studio

Depth of field area of a shot in sharp focus

dichroic mirror device for splitting light according to wavelength – used in video cameras to determine proportions of primary colours in a scene

digital recording encoding audio or video as numerical values instead of as a fluctuating electrical signal

diopter unit of measurement for the power of a lens. Colloquially used in TV for lens attachment making possible very large close-ups

director responsible for details of creative input to programme made by technicians, artistes, designers, etc.

dissolve gradual transition from one shot to another

dolly trolley for moving camera smoothly while shooting. Also used in US to describe the camera movement itself

dubbing mixing final sound track from recorded sound, commentary, music and effects; *also* putting different language on a programme

Edge numbers same as key numbers

effects (sound) recorded noise other than music or speech

emulsion coating on film making it sensitive to light – the less shiny side of the film which will stick to a moistened finger

encoding changing electrical signal from camera into form suitable for propagation

end board sync point marked by clapper board at end of shot

establisher general view (GV) of location

exposure amount of light allowed to fall on a frame of film; usually expressed as an f-number

exterior any out-of-doors shooting

eye-line the direction a person on camera is looking.

F-number the ratio between focal length and the diameter of the lens when fully open

field (video) area of TV screen covered by scanning alternate lines.
2 fields = 1 frame (picture)

filler light soft light used to fill out shadows

filters glass or gelatine lens attachments used to modify light entering camera

fine cut final stage in editing process

flicker irritating light loss between film or video frames – almost invisible at frequency of 48 or 50 per second

floor plan scale drawing of studio and facilities used to work out deployment of cameras, actors, etc.

focal length distance between lens and film surface or lens and video camera tube

frame complete video picture made up of two fields; a single picture on a roll of exposed film

freeze frame a single video field, or a film frame, displayed as a still on screen

frequency electrical term to describe number of cycles per second in alternating current (*see* cycle)

frequency modulation combining a signal with a carrier by modulating the carrier frequency

Gallery control room for studio

generation stages in copying videotape. The master tape is first generation; a copy of the master is 2nd generation; a copy of the 2nd generation copy is 3rd generation . . . and so on

grading adjusting light and colour in a previously exposed picture to obtain best possible quality

guest interviewee in studio

gun microphone highly directional mike

Hard light light throwing distinct shadow

head (video) electromagnetic device for laying down video signal on magnetic tape (recording) and reading the signal (playback)

helical scan scanning arrangement in which video tape is wrapped round the head drum in the shape of a partial helix, thus enabling tracks to be recorded diagonally on the tape

Hertz unit of frequency of repetitive electric current or voltage. One Hertz = one cycle per second

high-angle shot shot taken with camera above subject and pointing down

high-band version of U-matic video format

highlight brightest part of a picture

Insert editing assembling programme on videotape with prerecorded control track; replacing one video shot by another of identical length

interior any indoor scene

interlace video technique of scanning alternate lines of picture to eliminate flicker between frames (*see* field)

international sound track full music and effects track without commentary

interviewee person being interviewed

Jump cut a cut which violates continuity of time, place or action

Key light main light in a lighting set-up

key numbers numbers built into edge of film stock by the manufacturer to aid identification of shots. Automatically printed through on copies

Lacing threading magnetic tape round heads, automatically in cassette machines, manually in open reel machines

lanyard microphone neck mike

lavalier microphone neck mike

leader film stock at beginning of roll for lacing up, often with countdown numbers for accurate cueing

line-up retuning of electronic cameras before transmission or recording

location any place outside studio

long shot (LS) shot taken with camera at a distance from subject showing whole height of a person or the whole scene

low band version of U-matic video format

luminance black and white portion of the video signal

M & E track music and effects track

'macro' facility enlargement or close-up facility on most video cameras

medium close-up (MCU) comfortable close shot cutting just below armpits. Standard shot for TV interviews

microphone (mike) device for turning sound waves into electrical signal

mid-shot (MS) introductory shot for interviews cutting just below elbows

mix gradual transition from one shot to another

mixed light mixture of daylight and artificial light

modulate altering an electrical signal by combining it with another

monitor device for displaying TV picture without built-in off-air receiving facility

mute shot shot taken without recording sound

NTSC (National Television Systems Committee) TV colour system used mainly in North America and Japan

negative film (neg) original stock exposed in the camera. Light parts of the scene appear dark on neg, and vice versa. With colour neg, colours are replaced by their complementaries

Octaves a gradation of frequency. Each octave represents the span between a given frequency and double or half that frequency

off-line (video editing) a rough pre-edit on cheaper machinery to work out the best way of assembling a programme

omega wrap term describing tape path round helical scan head drum. Two types: open and closed. Named after Greek letter Ω

omnidirectional mike mike sensitive to sound from all directions

open reel magnetic tape not enclosed in a cassette which has to be laced up by hand

optical barrier imaginary barrier the crossing of which would result in crossing the line

opticals special effects such as mixes, wipes etc added to a film by the laboratory

PAL (Phase Alternate Line) TV colour system used in most of Western Europe except France

pan horizontal swing of camera

playback replay of video or audio recording

primary colours (video) red, green and blue, which can be added together in different proportions to produce any other colour

producer in overall charge of programme, especially organisation and finance

prop (property) any movable object used in a programme

protractor instrument for measuring camera angles. Used in conjunction with studio floor plan to plan shots

pulse signal to cue scanning beams in video camera and recorder

Quadruplex (quad) transverse scanning

format with four heads laying tracks across 2 inch tape

Radio microphone cableless microphone system fitted with tiny transmitter thus allowing user maximum freedom of movement

registration the term used for ensuring that the outputs of red, green and blue tubes in the camera coincide exactly when reproduced on screen

remote camera cableless video camera fitted with low power transmitter

reveal technique simple animation technique

reversal film film system which does without a negative

rock and roll dubbing equipment enabling sound track to be dubbed in short sections without audible joins

rostrum camera special mount for camera allowing smooth movements over stills, paintings, graphics, etc.

rough cut first assembly of shots during editing

rubber numbers numbers printed on edge of picture and sepmag after synchronisation but before editing

running order easy-to-change camera script for topical programmes

rushes film after processing before editing

SECAM TV colour system used mainly in France and communist countries

sepmag sound sound recorded or transferred to a *sep*arate *mag*netic track

set studio scenery

shooting ratio ratio of material shot to material shown

slow motion apparent slowing down of action in a scene: achieved in video by showing each field two or more times, and in film by running camera faster than normal

soft light light casting soft and indistinct shadow

spacing blank film stock added to picture or sound roll to fill gaps and thus ensure rolls remain in sync with each other

stops aperture settings on camera described by f-number

stripe *see* commag

sync (synchronisation) picture and sound exactly in time with each other

T-number (transmission number) f-number adjusted to take into account light lost while passing through the lens

talk-back continuous sound link-up between studio gallery and technicians involved in programme

telecine (TK) machine for showing film on TV

telephoto lens long focal length lens magnifying distant objects

teletext information display system transmitted in 'spare' TV lines at the top of the screen

tilt swinging camera upwards or downwards

time code system for numbering videotape

track moving camera forwards or backwards

transverse scan alternative name for quadruplex video recording

two-shot shot with two people in it

U-matic video format using ¾" (19 mm) cassette tapes; available in high-band and low-band versions

VCR Video Cassette Recorder

VHS (Video Home System) video format using ½" (12.5 mm) cassette tapes

VTR Video Tape Recorder

video used to refer to all aspects of electronic picture technology, as opposed to film

vignette 'keyhole' used in chromakey

vox pop technique of asking a succession of people for their views on one subject

Wide-angle lens lens with short focal length

wild track sound recorded on location independently from picture and therefore not in sync

writing speed speed at which video head passes across tape

Zoom lens with variable focal length

Index